Overcoming Common Problems

Coping Successfully with Acne

SALLY LEWIS

sheldon **PRESS**

This book is dedicated to all those who have been affected by acne

First published in Great Britain in 2009

Sheldon Press
36 Causton Street
London SW1P 4ST

British Library Cataloguing-in-Publication Data
A catalogue record for this book is available from the British Library

ISBN 978-1-84709-037-9

1 3 5 7 9 10 8 6 4 2

Typeset by Fakenham Photosetting Ltd, Fakenham, Norfolk
Printed in Great Britain by Ashford Colour Press

Produced on paper from sustainable forests

Contents

Acknowledgements

I would like to thank the people who helped me with the research for this book. In particular the British Association of Dermatologists and the British Skin Foundation, especially press officer, Nina Goad. To the complementary therapists, in particular Dr Peter Fisher, clinical director at the Royal London Homoeopathic Hospital, Trudy Norris, of the National Institute of Medical Herbalists, Don Mei at the AcuMedic Clinic and the skin specialists who answered my e-mails, including Professor Tony Chu, consultant dermatologist at Hammersmith Hospital.

To all the people who very kindly related their acne experiences, in the hope of helping others, thank you.

Also my thanks to Fiona Marshall at Sheldon for guiding me through this project, and, as always, my family – thanks to you all.

Introduction

Living happily in your skin can be very difficult if you have acne. Far more than a matter of 'a few spots', acne can appear overnight and devastate an individual's life. For teenagers, it comes at a time when they are finding their way in life, becoming aware of the opposite sex, being sociable and coming to terms with the changes in their body. Suddenly they are attacked by spots, zits and pus-filled red inflamed bumps that cover their face, shoulders, chest or back; self-esteem and self-confidence plummet, and they are plunged into a pit of despair.

Contrary to popular belief, though, acne is not just a teenage problem. While the peak age of onset is 17, recent years have seen an increase in the number of adults developing acne. In fact, acne can strike you in your twenties, thirties, forties and even – if you are unlucky – your seventies! For young adults, new job opportunities or relationships may feel jeopardized by a sudden unexplained outbreak of spots and a sudden loss of confidence. Or maybe you are pregnant and to your horror find your skin has erupted into a mass of spots, and you are then faced with the problem of trying to find a suitable treatment which doesn't affect your growing baby. Everyone with acne will ask: why me?

Acne is not just a skin disease – it can affect people on an emotional, personal, physical and psychological level. This distressing condition can dramatically affect self-esteem, sometimes leading to social avoidance and phobia, and even to depression. According to research, some 75 per cent of people with acne felt depressed as a direct result of having the condition, and an alarming 15 per cent felt suicidal. In some cases, acne may leave scars both mentally and physically, affecting some individuals on a long-term basis.

Acne doesn't just cause distress in the people it touches directly: it affects family and friends as well. Parents may struggle to understand the emotions and feelings of their teenager, as may the partner of the distraught pregnant woman dealing with an acne outbreak.

This book is aimed at anyone who has acne, or who is the parent, partner or friend of someone with acne. No matter what your age, whether you've suddenly developed spots or have been putting up with them for ages, this book is for you, in the hope that it will help you understand just what acne is, as well as what it is not. There are plenty of myths associated with acne, one of the most persistent of which is that it is linked with poor hygiene, and it's worth stating directly here that acne is not caused by a failure to wash! This book also looks at who acne affects and why, and the treatment options, from topical creams to the latest laser treatments. Lifestyle factors are also explored, including the role of diet and the benefits of exercise, and why it helps to control stress. The key point to bear in mind is that acne is treatable. It may take trial and error, and some persistence – many acne treatments take months to work – but the good news is that there is plenty you can do to tackle an acne outbreak, and on the way you'll probably be improving your general health as well. The goal of this book is not just to help you have better skin, but to help you understand the skin you have, and to live in it more happily.

1

Understanding your skin

If you have acne, having some understanding of the way the skin functions can help you understand your condition.

The skin is the largest organ of the body, with a surface area of approximately 2 sq. metres. It varies in thickness from around 0.5 mm on your eyelids to 4 mm on the palms of your hands and approximately 0.12 mm on your face. This amazing sensory organ acts as a shield, protecting you from damage, infection and drying out; it can also be an indicator of your health, with glowing skin being a classic reflection of well-being.

Skin is composed of two layers; the outer layer is known as the epidermis, and the fibrous inner layer as the dermis. Underneath the dermis lies the subcutaneous fat. The words 'epidermis' and 'dermis' derive from the Greek word for skin, *derma*; hence, a skin specialist is known as a dermatologist.

The epidermis is the thin waterproof layer, visible to the naked eye. It is made up of three sub-layers. The cells in the deepest layer of the epidermis – the basal layer – constantly divide, producing new skin cells and ensuring your skin is continually renewed and replaced. As these new cells are pushed upwards, so older cells nearer the top die. They rise to the surface of the skin, known as the stratum corneum, where they are filled with keratin, a hard protein which also forms the finger and toe nails. These dead surface cells are then shed, usually invisibly, by this continual process, which takes approximately 60 days to complete.

The dermis lies directly underneath the epidermis and is permeable, which is why injuries like burns and grazes 'weep' when the epidermis is no longer there as protection. The dermis is approximately four times thicker than the epidermis and is subdivided into two areas, the upper papillary region and the lower reticular region. It contains proteins, the most common of which, collagen and elastin, give the skin its strength and flexibility. Other components include numerous specialized supporting tissues, blood vessels, nerves, hair roots and sweat glands. The ducts of these sweat glands pass through the epidermis to the surface of the skin. In certain areas of the body specialized sweat glands – apocrine glands – develop after puberty. White blood cells, which help to keep the skin clear of infection, are also found within the dermis, along with fine hairs that rise from follicles. Along the side of each hair follicle lies the sebaceous gland, which produces an oily substance known as sebum. Sebum functions as a skin-softening agent (emollient), and as a protective agent against bacteria and fungi. When the sebaceous gland becomes inflamed or oversecretes sebum, the gland opening becomes plugged, resulting in spots appearing on the skin.

Subcutaneous fat layer

Situated beneath the dermis is the subcutaneous fat layer. Composed of loose, fibrous connective tissue, clumps of fat-filled cells, blood vessels and nerves, this layer has an important insulating role in regulating body temperature, one of the skin's most important functions.

Skin facts

- On average each 32 sq. mm (square half-inch) of skin contains:
  10 hairs
  15 sebaceous glands
  100 sweat glands
  1 metre of tiny blood vessels.

- The skin is thickest on the palms of your hands and the soles of your feet and thinnest on the lips and around your eyes.
- Your facial skin is approximately 0.12 mm thick and the skin on your body approximately 0.6 mm.
- The average adult's skin has a surface area of approximately 2 sq. metres and weighs around 3.2 kg.

(Courtesy of the British Association of Dermatologists)

The social importance of skin

By definition, the skin on your face is usually under constant scrutiny. Faces are one of the most important visual tools in communication and, justly or not, people tend to be judged by their physical appearance. Any condition which changes or alters the skin can affect the way others react to it. This is a major factor in people's experiences of acne. In a society where physical appearance is so important, anyone with facial skin disorders may be extra-sensitive to psychosocial rejection – even if it doesn't actually happen. Often, it isn't the severity of the acne itself which is the problem, so much as the severity of the person's psychological perception of the acne, or his or her reaction to having acne. An acute awareness that one's skin is 'atypical' does often militate against relaxed socializing, and in some cases even affects work prospects.

Acne vulgaris affects approximately 80 per cent of teenagers at some stage during puberty, so the majority of teenagers have to cope with any social stigma this entails, real or perceived. This may mean avoidance – for example, not going to parties or discos, or not joining in with sports, particularly swimming, when you have to undress and expose your body.

Many older individuals suffering from acne may also find their enjoyment and participation in daily social activities restricted. It is not just teenagers who feel anxious about their looks, although until recently the psychological effects of acne were thought to be not nearly so traumatic as for young people. But this view has now been rejected, as it has been better understood that acne can – and does – psychologically and socially affect an individual's quality of life. For the increased number of adults experiencing acne, it is clear that acne not only scars the skin deeper than in younger people but also equally affects the psyche. Many may lose self-confidence, become introverted and, in some cases, withdraw from others, not only socially but also from the workplace. Very often, over-obsession about their physical appearance and condition or state of their skin can lead to unresolved feelings of guilt, shame and embarrassment, as acne is often incorrectly regarded as a 'dirty' or 'unhygienic' skin condition. This social stigma does little to relieve the stress or psychological distress of the person with acne, who ironically is probably one of the cleanest members of society; many try to scrub away their spots, which only makes matters worse! What is more frustrating is the fact that acne can be treated, and early treatment helps to reduce the difficulties and suffering that may occur with this skin disorder. It is important to remember that the earlier acne is treated, the quicker and more successful the results.

According to the British Association of Dermatologists, attractiveness or beauty is considered to be 'a visual impression of form or colour'. While beauty can be subjective, in any one particular society there is generally agreement as to who or what is beautiful. Here in the Western world, the image of clear youthful skin and shiny hair is considered necessary in the quest for beauty. It is little wonder, then, that the beauty market, with its offers of creams, potions and lotions for wrinkle-free skin and clear complexions, is a growing multi-million-pound business.

Skin health

Your skin requires looking after, not just so that it is physically more attractive, but also because the healthier it looks, the healthier you are likely to be. Changes in the condition of your skin usually signify deterioration in your general health. A few spots or dry skin can be enough to suggest you are run down or suffering from stress, while sudden changes, such as dry skin, a change in skin colour, and cracked or sore skin, can suggest more severe health conditions.

A nutritious diet, regular exercise, good-quality sleep and fresh air will do much to promote the health of your skin, while water also plays an important role in keeping the skin healthy. Almost two-thirds of our body is composed of water – 83 per cent of our blood is water, 74 per cent of the brain is water, 75 per cent of muscles is water, and even bones are composed of 22 per cent water – but our skin is composed of 90 per cent. It is no wonder we are encouraged to drink eight glasses of water a day to keep ourselves hydrated. Tea, coffee and fizzy drinks may taste good, but too much caffeine (which is added to some fizzy drinks) may adversely affect you and dehydrate you further, affecting the efficient and smooth functioning of all your body's systems. Water helps to remove toxins and waste from the body, which makes your skin clearer, smoother and younger-looking. It literally moisturizes the skin from the inside out.

Most of the damage to skin, including pigmentation changes, thinning of the dermis, broken blood vessels and wrinkling of the skin, is caused by ultraviolet light, usually from the sun's rays. And while age may cause wrinkles, there is much that can be done to lessen its effects. Lifestyle factors such as smoking, poor diet, environmental pollution and over-exposure to the sun all contribute to damage and prematurely age the skin, and particularly the face.

So what is acne?

Acne is a very common skin disease or disorder, which comes about as a result of blocked and inflamed skin pores. It varies in severity from a few spots on the face that may be embarrassing and reduce self-confidence to a more serious problem that causes scarring. Acne usually starts in puberty. For the majority it lasts only a few years into the late teens or early twenties, but for some people it can persist much longer. It can affect people for the first time in their late twenties or even thirties, and in some cases occurs in babies.

Acne, also known as *Acne vulgaris*, is characterized by the appearance of comedones (blackheads and whiteheads), papules (infected spots) or pustules (pus-filled spots). Although there are several types of spot that differ in size, shape and colour, they all have one thing in common: they are all raised above the surface of the skin.

Why does acne occur?

Commonly, acne appears on the face, the neck, the chest, the back of the body and the arms, although it can appear anywhere on the body apart from the soles and palms. It is caused by a combination of factors, including

- the overproduction of sebum;
- dead skin cells clogging up the hair follicles;
- a reaction to the bacteria *Proprionibacterium acnes* (*P. acnes*).

Essentially, though, acne is a hormone-driven disease, with androgens (specialized male hormones) playing a leading role, though in most people with acne hormone levels are normal – the skin just over-reacts to them. What appears to happen is that the sebaceous glands of people with acne are more sensitive to normal blood levels of the hormone testosterone. Testosterone, which is present in both men and women, causes the sebaceous glands to overproduce sebum, a condition known as seborrhoea. At the same time, the dead skin cells lining the pores are not properly shed, so clogging up the hair follicles and blocking the pores on the skin. The effects can be wide-ranging, as pores can be found all over the skin except on the soles of the feet, the palms of the hands, and the lips.

The insides of pores are lined with skin cells known as keratinocytes. These microscopic lining cells live for a relatively short time and are continuously shed throughout your lifetime. When acne occurs, the pores become abnormally sticky through an excess production of keratin. The keratinocytes can no longer be shed one at a time, and this causes them to clump together, forming a plug of keratin and sebum (known as a microcomedone) in the hair follicle. These microcomedones then enlarge to form either an open comedone (blackhead), or a closed comedone (whitehead). The blocked pores trap the bacteria *P. acnes*, an unobtrusive bacterium found quite normally on every individual's skin, encouraging it to multiply and produce toxic chemicals. This triggers inflammation and inflamed spots (papules), although in some cases it produces inflamed pus-filled spots (infected pustules). If the blocked hair follicle erupts, then more inflammation occurs and may lead to the formation of cysts and nodules, which can ultimately scar the skin.

Who gets acne?

As a very common skin disease, acne is not selective, although in line with the onset of puberty *Acne vulgaris* tends to occur earlier in girls than in boys, peaking around the age of 13 for females and 15 in males. However, one study estimated that 14 per cent of women in the UK aged between 26 and 44 have facial acne. The study also demonstrated that the mean age of the population being treated for acne rose from 20.5 years in 1984 to 26.5 years in 1994, and that adult acne becomes less prevalent after the age of 44, when 1 per cent of men and 5 per cent of women will have the condition. A more recent study from Malta suggests that acne is even more prevalent in older people with 15 per cent of women and 7 per cent men over the age of 50 suffering from acne.

Adult acne can be broadly divided into two types: persistent acne, which is acne that has continued from the teenage years into adulthood, and late-onset acne, which presents for the first time after the age of 25. If acne is evident up to the age of 30, it is likely to persist until the age of 45.

Types of acne

Acne can affect all skin colours, and the process which causes acne is exactly the same for white or coloured skin. The impact, however, can differ according to skin pigmentation. A GP or a dermatologist can diagnose the type of acne you may have by looking at the types of spots and their distribution over your body. There are several types of acne, the most common being *Acne vulgaris*. Other types include severe *Acne vulgaris*, which falls into four types (*Acne conglobata*, *Acne fulminans*, gram-negative folliculitis and nodulocystic acne), and *Acne rosacea*. You may find that your acne is even referred to as 'teenage', 'occupational', 'cosmetically induced' or even 'drug-induced' acne.

Causes of acne

Acne is not determined by one factor. Generally there are several factors which together result in you having the condition; this is one of the reasons this skin disorder can be so difficult to treat. However, many of these factors can successfully be addressed and your acne can then be treated and controlled, if not cured. The causes include:

Genetics

There is a strong genetic link in families, so if one family member has had acne then the next generation are much more likely to have it too. Genetics can also determine when your acne is more likely to start and stop. However, this does not always follow, as some children whose parents did have acne may find themselves acne-free. While genetic factors do play a part in acne, therefore, they aren't fully understood, and it may be that other factors, such as lifestyle or environmental conditions, are required to trigger acne outbreaks.

Hormones

Acne is almost certainly caused by hormones, in particular androgens, which produce male characteristics and include testosterone. Both men and women produce androgens, although in varying quantities, and one of the contributing factors of acne is the stimulation of the sebaceous glands during puberty by the androgens testosterone and dehydrotestosterone (DHT), which ignite acne. Pre-pubescent acne is uncommon, as androgen production before puberty is minimal, while pubescent acne is most commonly caused by significant hormonal changes for both sexes. As adolescent boys naturally have more male hormones, including testosterone, they tend to be more affected by acne than girls during the teenage years. The constant flux of hormones during this stage may make acne difficult to treat, and it can often be the reason treatment needs to be varied. You may find that what works initially ceases to be beneficial and a different treatment is needed; this is all due to the hormones continually changing.

A very small percentage of acne occurs because of elevated androgen levels, a medical condition known as hyperandrogenism which can also lead to other health problems, such as heart disease, infertility and diabetes. Other signs and symptoms that may occur from abnormally high androgen levels in women include:

- excessive facial and body hair
- hair loss
- irregular periods
- deepening of the voice
- breast tenderness or discharge.

Acne arising from hyperandrogenism has to be treated in conjunction with the other underlying health problems; as a consequence, several specialists or consultants, including a dermatologist, may be involved in deciding upon treatment.

However, in most cases, although acne is caused by hormones acting abnormally, it is not due to abnormal hormones. As hormones play a much larger role in females' lives than in males', it is little wonder that acne is more prevalent in adult women. Generally, adult men's hormone levels remain relatively balanced throughout their lives, with a gradual decrease in testosterone as they age, although stress can affect their hormone production. Women naturally experience greater hormonal changes throughout their lives. Pregnancy and the menopause are both natural hormonal-changing conditions, while fertility treatment, the contraceptive pill and hormone replacement therapy (HRT) will all affect and alter natural hormone production. Even monthly menstruation can induce acne, and many pubescent girls – and even older women – will have experienced the dreaded spot or outbreak of spots just before a period. Women's hormones can also be affected by stress, increasing the chances of a break-out. While you may have had a successful response to over-the-counter treatments for acne during your teenage years, the chances are these will not help adult hormonal acne. Consequently, in all cases it is necessary for acne to be diagnosed by a doctor or dermatologist.

Typical signs of hormonal acne include

- an acne flare-up during pregnancy;
- acne that comes and goes with the menstrual cycle;

- acne associated with menopausal symptoms including hot flushes, mood swings, erratic or absent periods;
- increased stress from emotional or physiological causes leading to hormone stimulation and fluctuations.

Causes of androgen stimulation

Although hormones are naturally altered throughout a lifetime, there is evidence to suggest that certain lifestyle factors can stimulate androgens, causing them to overproduce. They include:

- stress levels – the more stress you experience, the more likely you are to increase your androgen levels;
- certain medical conditions, such as infertility treatment, where excess production of androgens occurs;
- hormone supplementation in foods – milk and meat products tend to be particularly affected;
- supplements, such as those in bodybuilding formula, which result in acne.

Stress

There have been several clinical studies that have identified stress as a major contributor to acne, in particular affecting existing acne. Stress affects acne in two ways: physical stress stimulates the adrenal glands to produce excess hormones, in particular testosterone, resulting in the formation of acne, while psychological stress is known to slow down the healing process of the immune system by up to 40 per cent, dramatically reducing the skin's healing ability. Not only can stress induce an acne outbreak, but it can worsen existing acne and affect the skin's overall condition.

Why and how it affects acne is related to the stimulation of the adrenal glands, which produce male hormones and androgens. It is these hormones, and particularly androgens, that stimulate the sebaceous glands, increasing sebum production and inflammation, which in turn results in the red, inflamed and pus-filled acne lesions so often seen on the face and skin of someone who is going through a stressful period.

Further studies published in *The Proceedings of the National Academy of Sciences* (2003) found that a chemical reaction probably exists between acne, other skin disorders and stress. According to these studies, during stressful situations the hypothalamus area of the brain releases a chemical known as corticotropin-releasing hormone (CRH). However, the oil glands of the skin also produce both CRH and CRH receptors, so when the CRH receptors come into contact with the extra CRH from the brain, excess sebum is produced, ultimately affecting acne and with direct consequences for the overall condition of the skin. As a result, individuals who have higher stress levels are more likely to suffer from acne and other skin conditions. So what is it that can create such a response in the body and bring about actual physical changes?

Stress is regarded as a 'physical, mental or emotional response to events that cause bodily or mental tension'. In what is known as the 'fight or flight' syndrome, the body automatically reacts to these responses by creating changes in hormone production and stimulating other chemical reactions within the body. These biological changes include the release of the stress hormones adrenaline, cortisol and norepinephrine into the body's system. The armed response is to determine whether we need to stand and defend ourselves or flee – it is what helped our Stone Age relatives survive the life-or-death situations they faced. However, today's modern living no longer requires what was once a survival necessity. Generally, we are dealing with daily psychological stress rather than real physical threats: the endless traffic jams, the constant juggling of family life and work, financial demands, the endless rushing around – all of these are what most of us would identify as stressful. And these daily and continual demands overload the body's system, making it more and more difficult to shut off. Even when the crisis is over the heart rate, stress hormones and blood pressure may remain high. It is readily accepted that stress has both physical and psychological implications, increasing and inducing health-related problems such as heart disease, insomnia, depression, obesity, high blood pressure and disturbed sleep patterns, and affecting mood, self-esteem, self-confidence and acne. In turn, acne almost certainly increases stress.

Smoking

Although it is widely recognized that smoking can cause lung or mouth cancer, heart attacks, strokes, emphysema and diabetes, it is not so well known that smoking can also cause acne. The nicotine constricts the internal blood vessels, reducing the supply of oxygen the skin needs to produce new cells and causing blocked pores and spots. More damaging, however, is the reduction in the blood supply to the skin and the consequent lessening of its ability to produce collagen and elastin, which keep the skin firm and smooth. A smoker will look older and age more quickly than a non-smoker, as the skin ages faster.

In fact, a smoker's skin is often the first tell-tale sign of the damage smoking is causing. According to the group Action on Smoking and Health (ASH): 'All over skin damage to the body occurs from smoking . . . over 4,000 toxins from a single cigarette are directly absorbed into the blood and transported into the structure of the skin, altering a person's appearance.' Researchers at the San Gallicano Dermatological Institute in Rome discovered a condition they called 'smoker's acne', characterized by blocked pores, and large blackheads which are less inflamed than those of *Acne vulgaris*.

According to the *British Journal of Dermatology*, women are particularly vulnerable to the condition. In a study of 1,000 women aged 25–50, 42 per cent of smokers had acne compared to 10 per cent of non-smokers, and smokers who had experienced acne in their teens were also found to be four times as likely to have the condition in adulthood than non-smokers who had experienced teenage acne. The research highlighted the fact that this type of acne, regarded as non-inflammatory acne (NIA), is common among smokers, with women who smoke four times more likely than non-smokers to develop NIA. Yet another good reason to stop smoking.

Bacteria

Acne is not an infectious disease. Therefore, although the bacterium *P. acnes* does play an important role, the bacterium alone is not responsible for acne, and neither does the severity of acne depend upon the number of bacteria on the skin's surface or in the hair follicles.

P. acnes is a normal bacterial inhabitant of the skin; it uses sebum as a nutrient, which is why more bacteria are present during puberty, when the glands become active. When the sebum becomes trapped within the hair follicle, the bacterium also becomes trapped and is able to grow unchecked, attracting white blood cells. This process triggers a chemical and enzyme reaction with the sebaceous material in the follicle that attacks and damages the follicle wall, allowing the contents to spill out into the dermis and causing an inflammatory response; red pustules, papules and nodules then appear under and on the skin. The bacteria break down sebum into fatty acids, which cause further irritation to the follicular wall, causing it to swell. Eventually, when the blocked follicle can no longer contain its contents, it bursts, spilling onto the skin. The process intensifies the inflammation, redness and pain in the skin commonly associated with acne.

The lesions will vary in severity, depending upon the damage to the follicle wall and the amount of inflammation present. Interestingly, although this bacterium may be acne-inducing – indeed, people with acne tend to have more *P. acnes* in their follicles than those without acne – it is thought that it may also have immune-boosting qualities, and may protect from other types of infections and even certain cancers. The fact that it is not fully understood why the hair follicles become obstructed – a process referred to as comedogenesis – is part of the reason a genuine cure for acne has so far evaded dermatologists.

Environmental pollutants and irritants

Environmental pollutants such as smoke, damp environments, other pollution and high humidity can cause or aggravate acne, as they block up and damage the skin. Very often these types of irritants can be work- or occupation-related. For example, if your job involves cooking or catering it may mean working in a hot and humid kitchen and you may find yourself with an outbreak of spots – or, if you are already predisposed to acne, you may find that your condition gets worse. Even the general pollution in your area can affect your acne: emissions from factories and refineries, the daily pollution from exhaust fumes and pesticides from gardens all contribute towards spots.

Medication

Very occasionally acne can be induced or affected by medication and drugs such as oral steroids. Even contraceptive agents, including medroxyprogesterone injections (Depo-Provera) and oral contraceptives, may aggravate acne, to the point where some women may find they have to change their contraception choice.

It is not known why some other medications cause or aggravate acne, but it is thought they all have a direct effect on white blood cells and the hair follicles. Medicines that are known to have an aggravating effect include anticonvulsant drugs for people with epilepsy, antituberculous drugs, antidepressants, lithium, halogens (iodines, chlorides, bromides, halothane) and vitamin B12.

Steroids, which are used to treat inflammation and auto-immune conditions, can also cause acne. Typically, acne from steroids usually appears in the form of papules, presenting mainly on the trunk; anabolic steroids, sometimes used by bodybuilders and athletes to build muscle bulk, are related to testosterone, the hormone known to affect acne. Both *Acne conglobata* and *Acne fulminans*, two severe types of acne, are common and very unpleasant side-effects of anabolic steroids. In most medication-induced acne cases, though, the acne only lasts for as long as the drug is taken.

Antibiotics and acne

Even certain types of antibiotics may cause acne. Antibiotics affect the digestive system, destroying both the good and the bad bacteria in the gut, and this in turn influences the body's ability to absorb essential nutrients, vitamins and minerals, leading to poor digestion and a build-up of toxins. If the body is unable to expel the toxins effectively through the kidneys, liver and bowels, it uses the skin and lungs. The result is often an outbreak of spots, which, like other medication-induced acne, will usually subside once the course of antibiotics is finished and the natural intestinal gut flora within the gut has settled. However, as antibiotics can be used to treat severe acne, this can sometimes lead to an antibiotic resistance to the *P. acnes* bacterium which is being treated. As a result, treatment options become more challenging.

Cosmetics

Acne cosmetica is a mild but persistent form of acne, characterized by small pink bumps. There may also be whiteheads and black-heads on the skin, which feels and looks rough. It commonly occurs on the neck, forehead, face, hairline and scalp. As the name suggests, it is triggered by the use of comedogenic (acne-producing) cosmetics, skin care and hair products. The cosmetic product stimulates abnormal growth of keratinocytes within the follicle, blocking it and creating a blemish. Cream blushers, eye creams, heavy make-up, heavy moisturizers, sunblocks and hair oil are often to blame. Applying more comedogenic make-up to cover the pimples will only make it worse.

Usually, you can determine which products are creating the problem depending upon the area of the break-out. For example, if the spots are around the eye area then there is a good possibility your eye make-up is to blame, while if pimples are occurring around your forehead or scalp then your hair products are more likely to be the problem. Small bumps all over the face and neck are much more likely to mean your foundation or moisturizer is to blame. Although it may initially be a case of trial and error, once the culprit is identified you can change to a non-comedogenic product and the problem should clear up relatively quickly. Luckily, because *Acne cosmetica* is so mild there is very little chance of scarring.

Polycystic Ovary Syndrome (PCOS)

PCOS is a hormonal condition affecting the ovaries, which may develop in teenage girls but can go on into adulthood, affecting women of reproductive age. Small cysts develop on one or both ovaries, which can result in infertility. Acne is a common and unpleasant symptom of PCOS, due to the production of excessive amounts of testosterone, which may be associated with increased facial hair. However, this type of acne responds well to treatment with cyproterone acetate, which is contained in Dianette, a contraceptive pill, though it does not respond well to other conventional acne treatments.

Charlotte only discovered she had PCOS at 16, after being treated for acne since she was 11.

Acne started in my first year at secondary school and it was awful. The spots got worse, especially along the jawline, which I now know is common when you have PCOS, and after six months I went to the doctor. He suggested several topical treatments, which included benzoyl peroxide, and at first the spots would clear up for a while but then come back. We spent the next four years going backward and forward to the doctor and I had several course of antibiotics, but still they didn't clear my acne.

Most of the time I dealt with it, until I began to get really upset in the fifth year when my friends and I were discussing the school prom. My spots were going to be more obvious than whatever dress I wore. The doctor suggested I tried the pill, as it was generally effective in treating acne, and I had some blood tests before starting treatment. It was then they realized I had PCOS and that my acne was probably linked to this condition. I didn't have a clue what PCOS was: although I had irregular periods this was put down to being very typical of my age, and I didn't have any other symptoms, so it was easy to see why they had missed it. I am now being treated with the pill, and after five months my acne is at last under control.

Keeping your weight under control is desirable, as being overweight increases the likelihood of developing this condition. Eating a healthy diet is recommended for women who suffer from PCOS, such as, for example, limiting sugary foods and 'white' carbohydrates, and eating wholegrain carbohydrates instead, plus small regular amounts of protein, fresh fruit and vegetables. Reducing stress often helps with the acne as well.

Diet

Only recently has research been able to link diet to acne, a factor that dermatologists and other health professionals had rejected for years. The connection between diet and acne is linked to the relationship between the types of foods consumed and the chemical changes that occur within the body at cellular level during the breakdown of food by digestion. Foods are also known to contain certain natural and synthetic hormones, and it is thought these disrupt the natural hormonal balance of the body.

Researchers found that a high glycaemic diet, typical of Western cultures (see p. 94), has a direct influence on blood sugar levels and increases insulin production, which is thought to make other hormones reactive. Milk – in particular skimmed milk, as it contains higher levels of whey, which is high in protein – naturally contains the bovine growth hormone, and this hormone is also thought to distort the natural balance of hormones within the human body. While scientists are in agreement about a direct link between acne and hormones, the understanding of what triggers the hormones to induce acne is still being researched; however, in the United States, where the majority of dairy products contain synthetically injected bovine growth hormone, scientists have been aware of this connection for some time. Leading US dermatologist Nicholas Perricone believes that foods which cause inflammation in the body, such as saturated fat in animal products and hydrogenated fat in processed foods, are directly linked to acne; he excludes all dairy produce and these types of fat as part of his acne treatment plan.

Sometimes a lack of nutrients is thought to cause acne. As the digestive system becomes depleted, so the natural bacteria in the gut (probiotics) are reduced and unable to process food and toxins properly. As a result, toxins are eliminated through the skin, causing skin problems including acne. Sugar, naturally found in most foods, increases testosterone production and produces an insulin response, which in turn creates inflammation and the insulin growth factor IGF-1, thought to induce acne in both men and women.

Insulin resistance

Insulin is a hormone that regulates carbohydrate metabolism and has an active role in protein and fat metabolism. When you are insulin-resistant, your body does not respond to the normal amounts of insulin released and blood glucose levels rise, causing an imbalance of blood sugar. The high blood sugar levels increase the levels of insulin and IGF-1, which increases the production of male hormones and androgens and encourages keratinocytes – the specialist skin cells implicated in acne – to increase. The pancreas, a gland organ in the digestive and endocrine system and an endocrine gland, produces several hormones, including insulin, and health problems occur when it cannot keep up with the demand for insulin. Over a period of time this will usually result in type-2 diabetes.

Low vitamin A and E levels

These are both fat-soluble vitamins, and necessary for healthy skin. Usually these vitamins do not need to be taken daily, as the body can store any excess for future use. However, many people who suffer from acne have been found to have low levels of both of these vitamins, which are so closely related that a deficiency in one will usually incite a deficiency in the other.

Vitamin E is thought to help prevent oil trapped within the pores from becoming hard and rancid, and lowers the chances of painful inflamed acne lesions, while at the same time repairing the skin. However, vitamin E reaches the surface of the skin via oil secretion from the pores: blocked follicles will prevent this vitamin from reaching the skin's surface, so that it is unable to lessen the inflammatory effects of the acne lesions. Vitamin A not only maintains the health of the skin but also strengthens the immune system. Its effects are similar to retinoids (see p. 54), and some conventional acne treatments, such as Retin A, are derived from vitamin A. Good food sources of these vitamins can be found in Chapter 8 on acne and diet.

Pressure and friction on the skin

This is a form of acne caused by heat, constant pressure, covered skin or irritation from repetitive friction against the skin. It is known as *Acne mechanica*, and outbreaks of acne occur wherever the irritation takes place. Wearing a helmet or chinstrap, for example, will enclose the skin, trapping the heat and causing irritation around the forehead or chin. Playing the violin for long periods of time can create an irritation to the neck; other irritations can be from shoulder straps, tight uniforms, head-bands and backpacks.

Acne grading

Acne can be classified as mild, moderate or severe. The grading is based upon the Leeds Acne Grading System, which grades from 1 (being the least severe) to 12 (greatest severity). Grading is based on the number of inflamed lesions and their inflammatory intensity, and is assessed by either a GP or a dermatologist.

2

Understanding your spots

Spots come in all shapes and sizes; they can be small and white, or large and inflamed. Some will affect the skin more than others, and some have the potential to damage and scar the skin. Acne spots are often referred to as acne lesions, as they bring about not only a physical change in body tissue but also a physical change in the skin. The types of lesions you have usually determine the type of acne you experience, and therefore affect treatment options. The most common lesions include blackheads, whiteheads, papules and pustules.

Types of spots

Comedones

A microcomedone is the precursor lesion of acne and is not visible to the naked eye. It takes approximately eight weeks for the microcomedone to develop into a visible non-inflamed acne lesion; these are referred to as comedones, and develop into either a closed comedone (whitehead) or an open comedone (blackhead). This is one reason why the full effect of acne medication is not achieved until treatment has been continued for several weeks.

A comedone is a sebaceous follicle plugged with dead skin cells, sebum, tiny hairs and sometimes bacteria. When the comedone is closed, the bacteria and sebum stay trapped below the skin surface, and at this stage it is commonly referred to as a whitehead because of its white appearance. Blackheads occur when the pore is only partially blocked, so some of the sebum, dead cells and bacteria are drawn to the surface. Contrary to popular opinion, the black appearance is due not to dirt but to the oxidizing of the substances in the pores, causing them to darken. Blackheads can take quite a long time to clear.

Macrocomedones are facial closed comedones (whiteheads), and are usually 2–3 mm or larger in diameter. Solar comedones appear on the cheeks and chins of older and elderly adults and are usually a direct result of prolonged sunlight exposure.

Papules

These are inflamed small (less than 5 mm in diameter) red tender bumps with no head. You may find a group of them in one area on the skin. They have a bumpy, sandpaper feel, but can be almost invisible to see. They are often referred to as pimples.

Pustules

These are very similar to whiteheads but are inflamed dome-shaped lesions. Appearing as red circles with a white or yellow centre, they consist of a mixture of white blood cells, bacteria and dead skin cells. Pustules are very common and are most often seen on the face, shoulders, back and breastbone. They can also be found in areas where excess sweating occurs, such as the armpits or the groin. Generally these pustules will heal without scarring if they do not progress to cystic form.

Macules

A macule is the red inflamed site left by a healed acne lesion. Luckily it is only temporary, although it may persist from a few days to several weeks or months before it disappears. If a number of macules are present at the same time, then they contribute to the 'inflamed face' appearance of acne.

Nodules

These are much larger than the other types of acne lesions already mentioned. Similar to papules, they are solid, dome-shaped or irregularly shaped lesions. Unlike papules, though, they can affect the deepest layers of skin with their inflammation. They can be felt as large hard bumps under the skin, and often are the result of a blocked sebaceous gland that bursts. The inflammation then spreads into surrounding tissue, where it damages the tissue and may lead to scarring. Nodules can be terribly painful and tend to last much longer than blackheads or pus-filled spots, usually for months at a time. These types of lesions can be very resistant to treatment.

Cysts

An acne cyst is a sac filled with liquid or semi-liquid material, consisting of white blood cells, dead cells and bacteria. Cysts have a diameter of 5 mm or more and are usually present, together with nodules, in a severe form of acne known as nodulocystic acne. Cysts can be very painful, and scarring is often the end result.

Types of acne

There are several forms of acne. The most common is *Acne vulgaris*, 'common acne', and typically the type most teenagers suffer from, although it can persist into adulthood. With this type of acne there are always whiteheads or blackheads or both, and many people have some experience of this form of acne at some stage of their life. However, there are different stages or categories of *Acne vulgaris*, which include mild, moderate and severe, and there are also several types of lesions. The individual lesions of *Acne vulgaris* are divisible into three types:

- non-inflamed lesions, which include open and closed comedones;
- inflamed lesions, which may include papules and pustules;

- scars: in most cases nodules are associated more readily with scarring, but cysts can also lead to scarring.

Mild acne

This is generally the type most of us suffer from at some stage, and if you are lucky and treat it early enough then it may well not develop further. Mild acne consists of several types of lesions, characterized by comedones, more often than not affecting the chin and forehead. Pustules and papules are rare but may be present.

Moderate acne

If acne does develop, it's often because treatment was not immediate. Although similar to mild acne in that it has comedones, papules and pustules, moderate acne is also characterized by more painful and deep-rooted lesions. It usually needs to be treated by a dermatologist to prevent it leading to severe acne.

Severe *Acne vulgaris*

This is characterized by deep-rooted inflammatory lesions, including nodules and cysts, which are painful and may cause scarring. If the inflammation is deep and severe or the spot is squeezed, it may burst deep inside the skin's tissue and spread inflammation, causing swelling and pain. The face and sometimes the body can be covered in lesions – not only is this painful but it can lead to psychological problems, including depression and loss of self-esteem. Very often this type of acne affects an individual's quality of life, including his or her social life and even employment.

Severe acne is much more difficult to treat than mild or moderate acne. It may last for years and requires aggressive treatment, but options are limited and treatment must always be by a dermatologist.

Other forms of acne

There are several other types of acne, including four types of severe acne, *Acne conglobata*, *Acne fulminans*, gram-negative folliculitis and nodulocystic acne.

Acne conglobata

The majority of those with *Acne conglobata* are men aged 18 to 30. It is a very severe form of inflammatory acne, and lesions are found on the face, chest, trunk, arms, back, buttocks, and even the thighs. Characterized by large lesions that often interconnect, it includes comedones, pustules and cysts filled with pus. Unfortunately, it causes wide-scale scarring due to the deep ulcers that form under the nodules and burrowing abscesses. This can sometimes lead to disfigurement and long-term damage of the skin, as well as psychological problems.

Acne conglobata can flare up after lying dormant for years. This form of acne requires expert medical care and is usually treated with isotretinoin (a derivative of vitamin A), corticosteroids and antibiotics. Several courses of treatment can be necessary over a period of years, and frequent routine check-ups by a dermatologist are necessary to look for signs of recurrence.

Acne fulminans

Also known as *Acne maligna*, this is another very severe form of inflammatory acne usually affecting teenage boys, but it can be also be seen in young adult males. It is characterized by a sudden acute onset of inflammation in existing acne, which can occur after unsuccessful treatment of *Acne conglobata*, and is accompanied by a sudden onset of fever, loss of appetite, atrophy and wastage of the muscles, and pain in the joints. In fact, this acne usually begins with pain and swelling in the joints, which then affects the lymph nodes in the neck. The lesions, which tend to appear on the face, chest and back, include inflamed nodules and cysts, which often become crusted and ulcerated.

Unfortunately, this form of acne can lead to extremely disfiguring scarring.

Acne fulminans is thought to be an immunologically induced disease, with elevated levels of testosterone, sebum and *P. acnes* bacteria. The treatment for this severe form of acne can be very aggressive, and may include hospitalization if treatment is not sought quickly. Isotretinoin, corticosteroids and non-steroidal anti-inflammatory medication to help reduce inflammation are the most suitable treatment options. However, the psychological damage from this type of acne may be severe.

Gram-negative folliculitis

An uncommon form of acne, gram-negative folliculitis is an inflammation of the follicles, giving the appearance of a pustular rash but with very few comedones or papules, and is caused by a bacterial infection. Because of its appearance it can often be mistaken for a flare-up of existing acne, and very often develops as a complication after long-term antibiotic treatment for *Acne vulgaris* or rosacea. The bacteria in this form of infection tend to be resistant to most types of antibiotics, and therefore a dermatologist will usually have to consider isotretinoin as a treatment option.

Nodulocystic acne

This form of acne is characterized by cysts that can occur singly or be widespread over the face, neck, scalp, back, chest and shoulders, and may be extremely painful. Unlike other types of cysts that are an abnormal dilation of normal skin structure, these are nodules of inflammation arising from an acne lesion. They are filled with thick yellow pus-like liquid and may need to be drained by a doctor when treatment is ineffective. When the cysts occur close together they produce a soft area undermined with tunnels, cell destruction and inflammation, resulting in *Acne conglobata.*

Treatment for nodulocystic acne requires antibiotics and isotretinoin, or in some cases intralesional corticosteroids that 'melt' the cyst over a period of three to five days. If this form of acne is left untreated, scarring may occur.

Adult acne

Unfortunately, acne doesn't confine itself to the teenage stage of life. Many adults find themselves experiencing acne, sometimes for the first time, into their mid-twenties and upwards. According to the British Association of Dermatologists, the median age of those with adult acne is now around 30, and acne persisting beyond the age of 25 is likely to continue for 10–20 years. Whereas teenage acne tends to present along the forehead, nose and chin, otherwise known as the T-zone, adult acne is more confined to the cheeks, jawline and neck, and the lesions tend to be deeper and more cystic.

It is not fully understood why adult acne is on the increase. Some dermatologists believe that more adults are developing acne, while others believe more adults are admitting to acne and seeking treatment, and a compelling case can be made for both theories – it is more than likely both are true. A recent study showed that 54 per cent of men and 40 per cent of women over the age of 25 are affected, although there are several theories as to why acne should be on the increase in adults. It may be due to small hormonal fluctuations that cannot be detected by routine blood tests. It is also possible that there may be an alteration in the responsiveness of the hair follicle, and/or a decline in serum levels associated with ageing.

Diet and synthetic hormones, found in food and the environment, are also thought to contribute to the increase in cases of adult acne, as is stress, a modern-day curse of our lives. Typically, work, a new job, exams and relationships during the period of life from the mid-twenties to the mid-forties are recognized as common stress triggers and play a major role in today's modern living. This tends to be a vicious circle – acne causes stress and low self-esteem, and stress aggravates acne.

Just as teenagers with acne may find it affects their social life, so too does adult acne affect the lives of older people. Only recently have doctors and mental health experts realized that acne suffered by adults is likely to have much greater long-term social, physical and psychological effects (including depression) than teenage acne. Dermatologists agree that adult acne is much more likely to leave physical scars: it is more prone to scarring than teenage acne, as the ageing process reduces the skin's collagen; scars will not heal as well as in young skin; and many adults are so self-conscious about their acne that they find it difficult to admit to it, and may not seek treatment until too late.

Tom, 34, admits to this problem.

I was finding myself in a new and challenging position at work after being promoted to manager of a department and expected to deal with clients and staff on a face-to-face level. Waking up with the odd spot wasn't too much of a problem, but by the time I admitted to myself that I was experiencing acne the spots had covered my face and developed into a red mass of inflamed spots. I was so self-conscious that I just couldn't face going into work. It was my girlfriend who persuaded me to see the doctor. She had bought some over-the-counter products, but I admit I didn't stick to the instructions very well. She told me I was becoming moody and had changed: we used to be very sociable but I was making excuses about being busy with work that I had to do at home in the evenings and at weekends – anything to stop us having to see anyone.

I went to the doctor one day after I had phoned in sick. He was really sympathetic and told me that the stress of my job had probably brought about my acne. I had had it quite badly as a teenager. He put me on a course of antibiotics, and within eight weeks I could see the improvement. He told me to take some exercise as well, to help me reduce my stress levels, so I took up jogging again.

I feel much better about myself now, and although my face is not completely clear it is so much better. I think it will eventually clear up completely. My girlfriend is happier, and we are back out seeing people again. I just wish I had done something about it sooner – the last year has been awful and it was unnecessary to suffer for so long.

If you were prone to acne as a teenager, then the chances are that acne is more likely to recur in later life. While the acne may not be as severe as during your teenage years, it's a hard fact that adult acne can sometimes be more difficult to treat – though not impossible. Luckily, more adults are now prepared to seek treatment for their acne rather than just putting up with it, so doctors are at last seeing acne as an adult problem. It's encouraging the medical world to take more notice of acne, helping to promote a greater awareness and new hope. For the best results, do make sure you visit your doctor as soon as possible. As with all acne, early treatment is effective treatment.

Adult female acne

Many women may find acne suddenly occurs during their twenties, thirties and forties, and although it is generally less severe than teenage acne it can be more challenging to treat. Female adult acne is characterized by comedonal acne on the forehead and cheeks, and inflammatory papules or nodules on the lower part of the face, chin and neck. While some women will continue to have persistent teenage acne, others who experience a sudden onset of acne may find it is due to underlying health conditions. A woman suffering from hyperandrogenism – the excessive production of androgen hormones – may have an abnormality of the endocrine system, which controls hormone production. This in turn can often be associated with serious health conditions such as infertility, heart disease and diabetes. Polycystic ovarian disease, where the ovaries do not function properly, may be another underlying cause of female adult acne. Stress is also an important factor in acne, according to experts such as Professor Tony Chu, consultant dermatologist at Hammersmith Hospital: stressed career women in their thirties and forties are typical of those who attend his clinics, desperate for treatment.

Perhaps, though, the most common reason for female acne is the constant hormone changes a woman experiences throughout her lifetime, which is hardly surprising when the relationship between acne and hormones is so closely intertwined. From puberty to regular menstruation, oral contraception (the progesterone-only pill is a common culprit of female acne), pregnancy and the menopause – these life events demand surges of hormonal changes that may trigger acne outbreaks. Typically, nearly half of all adult women find that spots appear a week before menstruation. The decrease in oestrogen and rise in testosterone before bleeding is thought to increase sebum production, while also increasing the size of the pores and stimulating the follicles to form acne.

Even pregnancy does not let you off the hook: just when you thought you might be entitled to the so-called 'bloom' of pregnancy, that glow is in fact due to the increase in hormones, which also increase oil production and hence spots. Indeed, for some women, pregnancy can be their first experience of acne. Of course, just because you are pregnant does not mean you will necessarily get acne – in fact, some luckier women find it actually clears up their regular acne! But for those who do experience acne during pregnancy, the first trimester, or first three months, is when spots are more likely to break out, not just on the face but also on the chest and back. Usually as the pregnancy progresses increased oestrogen levels help to clear up acne.

A few women will be unlucky enough to experience acne at both the start and end of pregnancy, because of the change in hormones as the body prepares for birth and raised hormone levels to sustain milk production for breast-feeding. The whole period is a hormonal roller-coaster, and little wonder that the hormones can spiral out of control. This process for some women may be repeated in further pregnancies.

Once the family is complete, a woman may need contraception, and the oral contraceptive pill Dianette is commonly prescribed to treat female acne. Pregnancy acne can be difficult to treat too, as many over-the-counter products cannot be used during pregnancy for fear of harm to the developing foetus. You must check with your doctor before using any products on your skin at this time.

Caution: if you already have acne and are planning to become pregnant, then you must discuss your treatment options with your doctor or dermatologist, as certain acne medications may be damaging to the unborn child.

As a woman ages, so her hormone production changes once again. The menopause, a period of time when hormonal changes occur and fertility diminishes, is well known for its hot flushes, mood swings, headaches, insomnia and loss of skin elasticity, but not nearly so much for its acne. It can be a challenging period for some women from the ages of 45 to 60, lasting years in some cases as the ovaries gradually decrease their production of oestrogen, sometimes erratically. The last thing you need as you get older is a case of menopausal acne, especially if you haven't had a spot since you were in your teens, yet this is just what some women experience, along with itchy, flaky skin, a skin condition known as seborrhoea and closely linked to acne.

It is thought that the decrease in oestrogen during this period of life is responsible for the outbreak, giving rise to an increase in androgens. Luckily, menopausal acne responds well to conventional acne treatments, especially vitamin A, but bear in mind that hormone replacement therapy (HRT), often used to help alleviate the other symptoms of the menopause, can sometimes cause an outbreak of acne. Best of all, menopausal acne tends to improve and disappear once the menopause is over.

Rosacea

Rosacea is a chronic, rash-like skin condition that can often look similar to *Acne vulgaris*, so sometimes causing problems with diagnosis. In addition, it tends to arise at the same time as an acne outbreak, hence making the condition even more difficult to diagnose. Unlike acne, however, there are no comedones; instead, it is characterized by its red, inflammatory appearance. Rosacea can cover the cheeks, nose, forehead and chin, causing swelling and red bumps, and the dilated blood vessels can become more visible on the skin's surface. Unfortunately, rosacea is often mistaken for flushing, and this appearance of blushing can add to the misery for those with the condition.

Although it affects both sexes, it is three times more likely to affect women, though it tends to cause worse symptoms in men. It can affect any age group, but is more common in the 30–60 age range. Rosacea has a hereditary link and tends particularly to affect people who are fair-skinned, with light hair and blue eyes. As well as affecting the skin, it can also cause other problems such as dry eyes and sore eyelids. Left untreated, it can sometimes cause swelling of the nose and the growth of excess tissue, resulting in a condition known as rhinophym, a bulbous nose. Because of this, and because of its similarity to acne, it is important for a doctor or dermatologist to diagnose the condition, as treatment for both skin conditions is very different. Do, however, remember that acne and rosacea can co-exist, so the doctor has to be vigilant in making the correct diagnosis.

Pyoderma faciale

Also known as *Rosacea fulminans*, *Pyoderma faciale* is a very rare form of acne that usually only affects females between the ages of 20 and 40. This unusual skin condition, found only on the face, cheeks, chin and forehead, is characterized by large painful nodules, pustules and sores. Unless aggressive treatment is immediately started, it may leave scarring. It can occur suddenly, sometimes overnight, without the person ever having had acne before, and although it is not fully understood it is thought to be a result of a severe reaction in which the hair follicles become engulfed in inflammation, thought to be induced by stress. It is often confused with severe acne and is deemed to be an explosive form of rosacea, but unlike severe acne it does not arise from comedones, and unlike rosacea it is not associated with blushing or flushing. Treatment often includes steroids, for their anti-inflammatory action. *Pyoderma faciale* usually lasts no longer than a year.

Corticosteroid acne

A side-effect of using oral steroids can be pustular acne on the face, chest, back, arms and thighs. Inhaled corticosteroids, such as those used in asthma inhalers, may also induce acne.

Acne cosmetica

As mentioned in Chapter 1, comedogenic cosmetic, skin, and hair products cause this form of acne, which results in small red bumps commonly found over the forehead, face, cheeks and neck. This acne is generally easy to treat once the product is identified and changed.

Acne mechanica

As we also saw in Chapter 1, this acne occurs from constant pressure, heat, covered skin and repetitive friction against the skin. For example, if you ride a horse or a motorbike or play sport where you are required to wear a helmet with a chinstrap for a relatively long period of time, then your head and chin will become hot and sweaty, and an outbreak of spots may appear on your forehead and chin. Soldiers may develop *Acne mechanica* on their backs and shoulders from carrying backpacks and equipment, and if they are posted to hot or humid environments the acne can develop further, becoming irritated and inflamed.

Musicians, particularly violinists, may find acne breaks out on their neck due to the violin being tucked and held against the neck for hours at a time; a similar effect can be caused by your mobile phone being held for long periods against your neck. Even underwear can cause acne: tight bra straps and tight pants can encourage spots on the back, thighs and bottom, and synthetic fabric will make *Acne mechanica* worse as it traps the heat against the body.

Acne mechanica spots can vary in appearance from small undeveloped microcomedones that are not visible on the skin but are rough to the touch, known as sandpaper acne, to inflamed pustules and papules. Luckily, *Acne mechanica* responds well to treatment, which usually includes removing the offending cause of the problem, but this is not always possible. However, *Acne mechanica* responds well to salicylic acid or benzoyl peroxide treatments and the wearing of cotton fabrics, but do consult your doctor if after several weeks of treatment it is still a problem.

Acne excoriee

Excessive scratching or picking at spots will result in this form of acne, which is often referred to as 'picker's acne'. Although tempting, squeezing spots does more harm than good and can leave scars and hyperpigmentation. It tends to be more common in females, particularly adolescent girls, and can be a sign of depression, anxiety or emotional problems. Often, what may begin as a mild form of acne becomes severe and prolonged from constant picking. It can be found on the face, back, chest, breast, back and upper arms. If the inflammation becomes infected, then the skin may become scarred. One of the distinguishing signs of *Acne excoriee* is hyperpigmentation of the skin: brown spots are the scars left on the skin from previous blemishes that have been picked to the point of tissue damage.

Chloracne

This is an acne-like condition characterized by blackheads, pustules and cysts, and the lesions are generally found on the cheeks, behind the ears and in the armpits and the groin area after exposure to chlorinated hydrocarbons, such as dioxins or PCBs. Direct skin contact with these chemicals, known as chloracnegens, and inhalation and ingestion are considered possible routes by which this acne develops.

Acne neonatorum or infantile acne

Newborn babies can get acne; some are even born with it, although it mainly affects babies from around the age of three to four weeks. In general, small whiteheads appear over the cheeks, forehead and chin, although there can also be red bumps or pimples or even nodules. It tends to be more prevalent in boys than girls. Testosterone passes from the mother's blood via the placenta and activates the sebaceous glands very early in foetal development. Babies are born with active sebaceous glands and therefore can develop acne. It usually settles down and disappears after a few months, generally between four and six months, but it is common for babies who suffer from this condition to have a tendency to develop acne again in their teenage years. Usually no treatment is necessary for this type of acne, and cleaning with oils and lotions may irritate the bay's skin further; however, as with all acne, the earlier it is seen by your doctor, the better.

Perioral dermatitis

Tiny papules, red bumps, pustules, yellow pus-filled spots and scaling of the skin are the main characterizations of this type of skin condition, which tends to affect young women. It usually presents around the mouth and chin, and may spread to the eyelids and forehead. Perioral dermatitis is very itchy and it is commonly mistaken for acne. While the cause is not clearly understood, dermatologists believe it is a form of rosacea. Strong corticosteroid creams used for other facial skin problems can cause perioral dermatitis, as can fluorinated toothpaste, facial creams, make-up and moisturizers.

Scalp folliculitis

Acne that develops around the scalp and hairline is known as scalp folliculitis. It is an inflammatory disorder of the hair follicles in the scalp. It is also known as *Acne necrotica miliaris* or proprionibacterium folliculitis. The scalp becomes dry, flaky and itchy; the itching is usually the main reason it is difficult to treat, as the lesions become sore and crusty from being scratched and are difficult to clear. *Acne necrotica* is a more severe form of scalp folliculitis and can affect other areas of the skin, including the face. It can also scar.

3

Day-to-day management of your skin

As acne is not a direct result of dirt, scrubbing at your skin will not improve your complexion. And don't think for one minute that acne is a sign of unloved skin: the chances are that you will have spent a lot of time, money and effort on treating your skin so far. Looks can be misleading. In fact, many people with acne will actually go to such lengths to cure their acne that they can create more problems for their skin – over-zealous cleaning can often lead to dry, irritated or inflamed skin. If your skin does become irritated, this may lead to the breakdown of the normal epidermal layer, resulting in the skin becoming open to infection from bacteria, fungi and viruses, and possibly causing further skin problems.

Back to basics

Cleaning

The best way to care for skin with acne is to treat it with a little gentle cleaning every day. It is advisable to cleanse the skin gently before using any form of topical medication – that is, medication that is directly applied to the skin. Steer clear of products that may be too astringent or drying for your skin.

In most instances, a non-perfumed foaming cleanser or mild soap is suitable for most acne-prone skin. Wash off the products with warm water and gently pat your face dry. It is best not to use a flannel, sponge or other kind of washcloth, as these can also irritate the skin and you may be tempted to scrub harder.

Cleaning the skin guards against infection and odours, but excess washing can easily dry it out, especially if you are already prone to dry skin, and may cause loss of oil in the outer layers of skin. Generally you don't need to clean the skin any more than twice a day, although the exception is if you get very hot and sweaty, such as after exercise, when it is worthwhile washing as soon as you can to help prevent further irritation and inflammation. If your hair is oily, or if you have scalp or forehead acne, then wash it regularly with non-comedogenic hair products. Remember, any hair products you use to style your hair, such as gel, may increase comedone formation.

For oily skin, using a gentle toner or astringent, ideally alcohol-free, to cleanse the skin is usually sufficient to remove surface dirt and dead cells. You can use a cleanser afterwards if you want, but make sure it is gentle and non-comedogenic. If your job or hobby means your face is covered with grease or oil, then use a non-perfumed foaming cleanser or mild soap and clean hands, rinsing off with warm water and patting your face dry. There are a number of over-the-counter soaps, creams, scrubs, lotions and gels for acne, most of which will contain the active ingredients benzoyl peroxide, alpha-hydroxy acids and salicylic acid; these are discussed more fully in Chapter 4.

Moisturizing

As many topical treatments can dry and irritate the skin further, apply a moisturizer regularly after use. Look for moisturizers containing glycerin, jojoba and linoleic oil, as they help to hydrate the skin. It is worth bearing in mind that glycerin does not suit all skin and may irritate the skin further, so if you feel your acne is getting worse then change the product. Bear in mind that the environment can make dry skin even drier – central heating, air conditioning and the weather can increase moisture loss, which in turn may lead to skin irritation, so do aim to moisturize on a daily basis. However, even if your skin is very dry, do not be tempted to overuse creams as this can increase oil production.

It is not just your face which may need moisturizing. If you have acne on the body then it is worthwhile moisturizing this too, especially after a shower or bath. And make sure the water is not too hot, as this can remove moisture from the skin.

Exfoliating

Whatever your skin type it is worthwhile exfoliating the skin, as this helps to remove dead surface skin cells which may clog the pores. Exfoliation is generally best done at night, after gently cleaning the skin. It is important not to overdo this treatment – twice a week is generally sufficient. And, as with cleaning, you should go gently and not rub too hard, otherwise you are likely to cause further inflammation and irritation.

There are two types of exfoliants, physical and chemical. The physical exfoliants include scrubs, abrasive pads, granules and natural ingredients, such as oat bran. Chemical exfoliants contain an enzyme or acid, such as alpha-hydroxy acid and beta-hydroxy acid, which loosens the skin's dead cells; they are generally more suitable for acne skin.

Tea tree oil is an alternative face and body wash for acne-prone skin. An essential oil of the Australian native tree *Melaleuca alternifolia*, it is known for its antibacterial, antifungal and antiseptic qualities. It has been compared to benzoyl peroxide for helping to combat acne, and research has demonstrated that in treating moderate acne, 5 per cent of tea tree gel, compared with 5 per cent benzoyl peroxide, has a significant effect in reducing inflammation and comedones. It has also established that tea tree gel has fewer side-effects than benzoyl peroxide. However, undiluted tea tree oil should not be applied directly to the skin, as it can cause irritation, redness, overdrying and blistering. A tea tree oil solution of 5 ml tea tree oil to 95 ml water is recommended, or tea tree gel can be bought over the counter.

Skin health

Skin needs to be healthy on the inside to be healthy on the outside, so a good, nutritious diet with plenty of fruit and vegetables is recommended. Cutting back on sugar, carbohydrates, fast food and caffeine is beneficial. Fresh air and sunshine help too, but remember to use a sunscreen (see p. 42). Water helps to maintain hydration of the skin and improves the complexion, and giving up smoking will improve not only your skin tone but also your overall health. All these lifestyle factors will help to give your skin the best possible chance of staying healthy.

Acne in other places

It's not just the face that can succumb to acne: the chest, back and even the buttocks can suffer too. The reason for an outbreak in other areas is generally similar to facial acne – an abnormality in the overproduction of sebum. However, very often clothing, perspiration and friction may irritate skin and cause a break-out of spots. Treating acne elsewhere on the body does not differ from treatment for facial acne, though a few other factors may need to be considered as well.

- The chest is generally more sensitive than the back or buttocks to antiseptic washes, and irritated skin or a rash may occur if the treatment is too harsh.
- It's helpful to wear loose-fitting clothing, which won't chafe the skin.
- Washing more regularly to help get rid of perspiration, for example after vigorous exercise, will help stop irritation of the skin – though, as always, be gentle and don't overdo it.
- Applying medication such as benzoyl peroxide to your own back can be difficult, so if you suffer from back acne ask one of your nearest and dearest to help.
- Bear in mind that scrubbing at the skin with a loofah or similar can also cause inflammation. A simple gentle cleaning

product can be used, and the body should be patted dry with a towel, rather than rubbed, afterwards.

• Apply a non-comedogenic moisturizer to the body after washing, just as you would with facial acne.

• Rucksacks and backpacks can often irritate and rub the skin on the back and shoulders, and should be removed if an outbreak of spots occurs.

• The buttocks are particularly difficult to clear from spots, especially if you have to sit down for most of the working day. Again, avoid tight-fitting clothes. All clothing, including underwear, should ideally be made from cotton or other light breathable fabric.

Sunscreen

Being outside in the sunshine not only improves your well-being but also helps the body to manufacture vitamin D, enabling the absorption of calcium and improving bone health. However, it is important to protect yourself from the sun's harmful ultraviolet A (UVA) and ultraviolet B (UVB) rays. These rays have the potential to burn the skin and cause rashes and prickly heat. Sunburn is also implicated in skin cancer (for more details, see *Skin Cancer: Prevent and Survive* by Dr Tom Smith, Sheldon Press, 2006).

While small amounts of exposure to the sun can help to improve acne, unfortunately sunlight can also worsen it. Striking a balance can be difficult. Too much exposure to the sun can cause sunburn, which will irritate your skin and increase the acne. The skin's surface thickens and the dead skin cells won't exfoliate as quickly, leading to more blocked pores and more spots.

Choosing the right sunscreen is vital when you have acne. Sunscreens are, unfortunately, a common cause of acne breakouts.Oil-free non-comedogenic products, with a UVA and UVB minimum factor of 15, are advisable, and you may find gels more suitable than creams. It may be worth gently cleaning your skin before you apply your sunscreen, and although your acne may be irritated or even break out after using your sunscreen, it is always advisable to wear it.

Some acne medication, such as antibiotic therapy, makes the skin more susceptible to the sun's rays, and in these instances it may be necessary to apply sunscreen on a daily basis. Be careful not to consider moisturizers with sunscreen as suitable protection, as many have minimal effect. Your GP or dermatologist should be able to advise you on this when providing you with your acne medication. If you are using topical retinoid treatment, apply your sunscreen directly afterwards.

Remember: only use these at night and wash off in the morning. They are photosensitisers and make the skin more sensitive to the sun, so it is important not to go out in the sunshine with the retinoid on.

For acne-prone skin, the British Association of Dermatologists recommends applying factor 15+ sunscreen, with broad-range spectrum protection from UVA and UVB rays, every two hours, even if there is partial sun or cloud cover. It is also advisable to apply sunscreen more frequently if you are swimming, or perspiring heavily. If exercising outside you may be more prone to sweating, but be careful not to apply too much sunscreen to your forehead, as any excess may run and drip into your eyes, causing irritation.

Be careful not to use sunscreen or moisturizing products containing lanolin, a by-product found in sheep's wool. This is very oily and known to affect acne skin adversely, especially in those whose acne is genetic.

A suntan may give the appearance of health. Indeed, much emphasis in the Western world is placed on the golden colour of skin, and some people will go to extremes to achieve a tan, from excessive sunbathing to sunbed use. The British Association of Dermatologists does not recommend sunbeds. It is thought that they give little benefit and may have potentially damaging effects on the skin. Remember, the more you look after yourself, the healthier your skin will appear.

Facials

While there is no guarantee that a facial will improve your acne, people with mild acne may find they benefit from a professional facial, especially if done regularly. If your acne consists mainly of blackheads or whiteheads and is non-inflammatory, then very often a facial will produce good results. During a facial the skin is cleaned thoroughly, and manual extractions may be performed to clear blocked pores. Mechanical extraction of comedones is not, however, without its downside, as scarring may occur if this is too vigorous. Steam should be avoided as steam from facial saunas, steam rooms or conventional saunas can induce acute blockage of the pore by swelling the microcomedone and this can result in an acute breakout of acne. Facemasks and facial massage may also be incorporated into the treatment, and moisturizer applied to soothe and hydrate the skin.

If your acne is moderate to severe, with nodules or cysts, then consult your GP or dermatologist for advice first, particularly if you are using topical or oral medication such as Accutane or Retin A, as these forms of acne should not be treated with facials.

Usually facials are carried out at beauty salons by qualified therapists who should be able to offer a suitable facial for your acne, but if you are unsure it is worthwhile discussing this with your dermatologist, who may be able to recommend someone for you.

Shaving

'Shaving bumps', otherwise known as *Pseudofolliculitis barbae*, are not acne but a persistent inflammation of the skin caused by shaving. After the hair has been shaved it sometimes curls into the skin as it regrows, causing an inflammatory reaction. This form of acne tends to occur more in males with curly hair. Treatment includes allowing the beard to grow for a period of three to four weeks or, if this is not possible, shaving every other day, which will also help to improve the condition. The use of an alcoholic solution containing 1 per cent clindamycin has been shown to be effective in treating this condition, when it is used immediately after shaving.

While shaving itself does not cause acne, certain factors, such as using the wrong shaving cream or blade for your skin type, can irritate or cut the skin, causing infection and an acne-like rash. If the skin has been cut, it is worth changing the razor blade daily to prevent cross-infection. Not shaving if you don't have to will help the skin to heal. Using a tea tree-based shaving gel, or one for sensitive skin, may help to lessen the inflammation, and although it may be difficult, try not to shave over the spots for a few days. Electric shavers also need to be cleaned regularly to prevent infection. Experimenting with a wet and a dry shave, to see which works best for your skin, is also worthwhile. The shaving products you use should be alcohol-free, as alcohol-based products will not only dry the skin but can be painful if applied directly to the spots. Moisturizing after shaving will help to keep the skin hydrated but, again, use non-comedogenic moisturizers.

Cosmetics and fragrances

It is thought that up to 30 per cent of skin cosmetic users have acne-prone skin, which is why cosmetic acne is on the increase in the Western world. *Acne cosmetica* results in small red spots or bumps that can last from a few days to several months. Sometimes it occurs as a reaction to a new skin product, or because the products are comedogenic. Cosmetics may also be labelled 'oil-free', but synthetic oil substitutes may affect acne-prone skin because of the chemicals they contain, such as stearic acid and isopropyl myristate. These chemicals are often added to cosmetics products and skin lotions to give them a sleek, sheer feel. Other chemicals to avoid in cosmetic products include isopropyl palmitate, isopropyl isothermal, putty sterate, isostearyl neopentonate, myristyl myristate, decyl oleate, octyl sterate, octyl palmitate, isocetyl stearate and PPG myristyl propionate. Crude coal tar, lanosterin, sterolan, and D and C red dyes, common in blushers, should also be avoided.

If you suffer from this condition, it is best to use non-comedogenic cosmetic products. Ideally, make-up should not be worn every day. When you do wear it, it should be removed as soon as possible, while make-up brushes are best washed regularly in mild shampoo and thoroughly dried. If your acne is over your forehead and in your scalp, change your hair products to non-comedogenic products and try to keep them away from the skin at the front of the hairline until the spots have cleared up. To help clear existing spots, exfoliate regularly and use a cleaner or make-up removal wipes with salicylic acid. However, as with any form of acne, if you have changed all your products and the spots are still there after six to eight weeks, then see your doctor.

Fragrances found in cosmetics and hair products can cause skin reactions and adversely affect acne skin. Even fragrances applied directly to the skin may cause a reaction which can lead to the development of acne. Cosmetic products labelled 'unscented' may still include fragrances to mask the smell of other ingredients. Products labelled 'fragrance-free' or 'hypoallergenic' are more suitable. The most common acne-inducing fragrances are bergamot, ambrette and the musk family.

4

Conventional treatments

It's important – though hard sometimes – to keep acne in perspective. At some time everyone will have a spot or two: it's normal to have a few spots breaking out. However, if they persist, or more develop, then it really is worthwhile making an appointment to see your doctor, who will be able to determine whether you have acne, and if so which type, as this will help you to decide on the best treatment available.

There are numerous over-the-counter products for acne. Some offer a 'quick-fix' solution, but do be aware that in most cases acne is not something that can be cured overnight. Because of the complexity of acne and the numerous reasons for its occurrence, most successful acne treatments have to be continued for many weeks before improvements can be seen. The successful treatment approach varies from person to person, as each individual's skin is unique. Therefore, a treatment which might work for one will not necessarily work for another. Even your age may be a factor in determining how long your acne lasts and how your skin reacts to one product. Some individuals may have to try several products before they find the one most suitable and successful for them. Bear in mind, too, that most products take 8–12 weeks before improvement can be seen. Rather than prolong the period of trial and error, it is more effective, both physically and emotionally, to make an appointment to see your doctor. He or she can advise you on the best treatments for your skin and your acne type, which may also include prescription medication.

Before you begin

Before you see your doctor, it is worth knowing as much as you can about your acne. This will help you, and your doctor, to choose the most suitable medication.

- Draw up a daily acne log. You need to chart your spots. Counting spots can be difficult, so always start on the same side of the face.
- Keep a chart of your skin. You may find it changes during the month, or it may be oily in certain areas, such as the T-zone, along the forehead and nose, and dry in others.
- Identify any other factors that make your acne worse. For example, if you know stress affects your skin and there are reasons for the increase in your stress levels, you can identify a pattern to your acne outbreaks.
- Do ask your doctor to tell you which type of acne you have. This way, you will have a better idea of which types of treatment are suitable.
- Make sure you understand how long your treatment should be used for, and then follow it up with another appointment so you can determine how successful the treatment has been.
- Ask what treatment will help stop new lesions from appearing.
- Make sure you decide the course of action that suits you; it is no good agreeing to a treatment if you know you won't follow it through for the required period of time.
- Inform yourself about the side-effects of any medication you are offered.
- Realize your treatment may last months, in some cases even years.
- Understand what you need to do in order to help prevent acne from scarring your skin.
- Continue your daily log for as long as your medication is prescribed.

- If you feel your acne is not responding to treatment, ask to be referred to a dermatologist.

Over-the-counter products

The most usual treatment for mild acne generally begins with over-the-counter products available at a pharmacy or super-market. Any treatment applied directly to the skin is known as a topical treatment, and includes washes, gels, solutions, creams and ointments. Most of these will contain one or more of the active ingredients benzoyl peroxide, alpha-hydroxy acids and salicylic acid. Topical treatments must be applied to all the skin, not just to the spots. They must also be continued, even if the acne is clearing up, for a period of time afterwards, to keep the lesions under control.

Choosing your treatment comes down to your skin type, the type of acne you have and its severity, and your own personal preference. Washes, for example, are quick and can be used in the shower, and while they are sometimes slightly drying they rarely cause any irritation. In general, creams and ointments tend to be more moisturizing, so they are good for dry and sensitive skins. Gels and solutions are more suited to oily skin, particularly as they help to dry out the skin. Ointments can be very greasy, so they may be more suited to those who prefer to use them at night, and a wash, gel or lotion in the morning.

Combination treatments, when one agent is used in the morning and another at night, tend to be much more suc-cessful, especially with regard to adult acne. However, it can take several attempts to find the right combination for any signifi-cant improvement of the skin to take place. Very often doctors will prescribe a topical treatment containing an antibiotic combined with benzoyl peroxide or zinc in order to improve its effectiveness. Many teenagers find these combination types of products the easiest to use, as they are less willing to adhere to strict regimes where a combination of treatments is given.

The most common side-effects of over-the-counter products include the drying or irritation of the skin. Excessive redness, itching or burning are possible signs of an irritant reaction, so either go back to the pharmacist or see your doctor as soon as you can, and stop the application of the product immediately. As treatment can take several weeks before an improvement is seen, any disruption will increase the length of time it takes.

Acne treatments are categorized into those that:

- kill bacteria;
- normalize pore lining cells;
- decrease inflammation;
- exfoliate;
- alter hormones or hormone effects;
- decrease oil gland production;
- use laser, ultraviolet and intensive light therapies.

Treatments that kill bacteria

There are a wide variety of treatments which kill the bacteria in the pore and on the skin.

Benzoyl peroxide

The most common bacterial treatment for acne, this active ingredient is found in most over-the-counter products. An antimicrobial agent, benzoyl peroxide releases free oxygen radicals in the sebaceous follicles, ensuring bactericidal activity against the acne bacteria, *P. acnes* (which is anaerobic, meaning that it will only grow in the absence of oxygen). It also helps to unblock the pores and decreases microcomedone formation, at the same time drying up greasy skin. It is useful for treating blackheads, whiteheads and red inflamed spots, and can be applied directly to the spots. It is worth noting that this treatment works best if it is applied 20–30 minutes after you have washed your skin.

Benzoyl peroxide is an active ingredient in prescription medication, and is available in 2.5 per cent, 4 per cent, 5 per cent and 10 per cent concentrations. You need to find the strength that suits your skin as the higher concentrations do have significantly more side effects.

Brand names for benzoyl peroxide include Brevoxyl and PanOxyl. Benzoyl peroxide can be combined with an antibiotic, clindamycin, whose brand name is Duac Once Daily. A prescription from your doctor is required for this.

As with any medication, there are side-effects, and benzoyl peroxide typically causes drying of the skin or irritation. Keeping to the lowest preparation, 2.5 per cent, may help, and using a water-based preparation rather than an alcohol-based one helps to reduce these effects. You can also limit applications to once a day until your skin becomes more used to the product, washing off the solution after several hours and gradually increasing the amount of time you leave the preparation on your skin. Your aim is to use the treatment twice a day. Benzoyl peroxide can also induce redness, peeling, burning or itching, and through its bleaching effects can discolour clothes and bedding, especially when applied to the chest or back. Precautions such as wearing a cotton T-shirt in bed and changing your pillowcases should be taken if you are planning to leave the treatment on overnight. It is wise to avoid direct sunlight when using this product, as you may find it increases your sensitivity to the sun, increasing the chances of sunburn and sun damage.

Salicylic acid

Salicylic acid is a beta-hydroxy acid, with antibacterial and anti-inflammatory qualities. It is a key ingredient in many acne treatment products, often combined with other agents including zinc, sulphur or coal tar. It comes in gel, ointment, shampoo or liquid form. Common examples of this treatment include Clearasil, Neutrogena Rapid Clear and Clean and Clear.

Azelaic acid

Azelaic acid not only helps to destroy bacteria, but also helps to reduce the growth of keratin (surface skin cells), unblocks pores and sebaceous glands, and reduces the formation of comedones. Skinoren cream is a prescription-only preparation containing azelaic acid and should be applied to the affected areas twice a day, except for those with sensitive skin, who should only use it once a day. Regular use is important, and after four weeks there should be some visible signs of improvement. According to the manufacturer, the cream should be used for a period of several months, but not more than six months, for maximum effects. It is often used as an alternative if benzoyl peroxide or topical retinoids cannot be tolerated.

Topical antibiotics

As well as killing bacteria, antibiotics help control inflammation. Antibiotics can be used alone or with other topical acne agents. The drugs erythromycin (Benzamycin gel), and clindamycin, (Duac Once Daily gel), for example, are both used with benzoyl peroxide. These antibiotics can be found in gels, washes, creams, lotions, ointments and solutions.

Topical antibiotics are always preferable to oral antibiotic medication, as they have fewer side-effects or allergic reactions and can be used twice a day.

Oral antibiotics

Despite good skin care, sometimes topical treatments are not enough to control acne, and oral antibiotics may be prescribed. They include the tetracyclines (oxytetracycline, lymecycline, minocycline and doxycycline), macrolides (erythromycin and clarithromycin), and trimethoprim. They are generally prescribed for mild or moderate acne not responding to topical treatment. Occasionally the acne can start to become resistant to a type of antibiotic, and it may be necessary to change to another.

The side-effects of oral antibiotics can be more severe than for other treatments, and can include sensitivity to sunlight. Oral antibiotics can also affect the effectiveness of the contraceptive pill for up to 3 weeks after starting it, so extra precautions may need to be taken for this period of time. Usually oral antibiotics and Retin A, a retinoid treatment which helps to normalize pore lining cells, are prescribed together to ensure the best results.

Corticosteroid injections

Very occasionally, the injection of corticosteroids into an inflammatory cyst or nodule can dramatically decrease its size, although a repeat injection two to three weeks later may be needed. It is a form of treatment that is used for acne that flares up now and again, as an additional treatment when the acne cannot be completely suppressed by oral antibiotics or isotretinoin or if you are unable to consider isotretinoin treatment. Once the cyst or nodule has been injected, the skin will flatten out.

Acne surgery

This is the term used when the closed comedones are opened and the contents expressed in the hope of speeding up the resolution of acne. Very often, purulent nodules can be incised and drained of pus. There are various types of comedone extractors; each is a small instrument that applies pressure to the surface of the comedone. However, this treatment is rarely used by doctors now as topical retinoids are a much more popular option.

Treatments that normalize pore lining cells

The most important category of these treatments includes retinoids, which are vitamin A-based medications. Topical retinoids include tretinoin (Retin A), adapalene (Differin) and isotretinoin (Isotrex), and are available in different formulations and concentrations. They have been found to be effective for mild to moderate acne, reducing the number of inflamed and non-inflamed lesions in 8–12 weeks. According to research, adapalene and tretinoin are proven to be effective in reducing inflammatory acne by 47 per cent and 50 per cent respectively, and non-inflammatory acne by 57 per cent and 54 per cent. Adapalene is significantly the more effective of the two, benefiting two out of three people.

Retinoids work by normalizing the follicular lining cells, loosening the cells in the skin and unblocking the pores, allowing the natural oil-producing glands to work properly. They also help decrease inflammation and act as a natural exfoliant, removing dead skin cells.

The gel is considered more suitable for oily skin, and the cream for dry skin. These products can be bought over the counter, but generally those prescribed by a doctor are more effective, as they have a higher retinal concentration level.

Initially when these products are used they may turn the skin red or irritated, which is often the reason so many people stop their treatment, mistakenly believing this sensitivity to be an allergy or an adverse reaction to the product. However, most people find that with regular use these effects subside, and in most cases the treatment goes on to be very successful. Tretinoin has more adverse effects than do other topical retinoids. There are some other side-effects with retinoid treatments, which include an increased sensitivity to the sun and UV light, but your doctor or dermatologist will offer guidance if you use this product.

Adapalene (brand name Differin)

Adapalene is a retinoid-like drug and affects the growth of skin cells, reducing the production of keratin. It is more suited to those with dry or fair skin, and is available in a gel or cream form. The cream is less irritating than the gel and thus suitable for sensitive skin, but less effective in comedonal acne.

Isotretinoin

Regarded as the most effective retinoid acne treatment, isotretinoin is available as a gel (Isotrex gel) or in the stronger oral form; in the UK the most widely prescribed form is known as Roaccutane. Capsules are only available on prescription, and can be supplied by your dermatologist. If you are a woman of childbearing age, European legislation means that you can only be prescribed the drug for 30 days at a time and will be checked to make sure you are not pregnant before a further prescription is given.

Isotretinoin is considered to be the best treatment available for treating severe acne that has not responded to conventional treatment and/or oral antibiotics. It takes at least six to eight weeks before a beneficial effect can be seen, and in the first seven to ten days the acne can actually get worse. The drug should be prescribed until all spots are clear and for a minimum of four months and you will be kept under close supervision during this time. In most cases the acne will completely clear up, and skin may remain acne-free for some considerable time. It is not always a cure for acne and 50 per cent of people will relapse some time after the treatment is stopped.

Isotretinoin is an anti-inflammatory agent derived from vitamin A and works by reducing the size and activity of the sebaceous glands in the skin, which reduces the production of sebum. It prevents the glands from becoming blocked, so that bacteria are unable to thrive, and it reduces inflammation.

This drug does have a number of side-effects, which include drying of the skin, aching joints and muscles, lip soreness and reddening, and scaling of the skin. Some severe side-effects of this drug include depression, which has been associated with suicide. You cannot use this treatment if you are pregnant or considering becoming pregnant as it can cause major deformities for the foetus. Should you require further treatment then at least eight weeks have to pass before you can start another course. Oral isotretinoin also reduces skin healing and increases skin fragility so operations and laser treatment of the skin should be avoided for 6 months after stopping the drug and while on treatment, women should avoid waxing.

Treatments that decrease inflammation

Red bumps and tender red spots are a direct result of inflammation, which can lead to scarring. Controlling inflammation is a necessary part of acne treatment. Antibacterial agents, such as benzoyl peroxide, salicylic acid and retinoids, all demonstrate some anti-inflammatory properties, but oral antibiotics are even better at controlling inflammation. The inflammation occurs as the body's immune system reacts to increasing levels of *P. acnes* in the follicle.

Treatments that exfoliate

As clogged pores play such a major role in acne, removing the dead skin cells and unclogging the pores is an important approach to treatment. With acne-prone skin, the process of producing and removing dead cells becomes abnormal. Dead cells build up on the surface, preventing moisture, oxygen and nutrients from reaching the new cells that are forming underneath. Exfoliation using alpha-hydroxy acids, beta-hydroxy acid or microdermabrasion can be used.

Alpha-hydroxy acids

Naturally occurring organic fruit acid and water-soluble alpha-hydroxy acids (AHAs) are available in many cosmetic products, including cleansers, toners, moisturizers and chemical peels. Applied topically, they increase the rate of cell turnover, decrease the stickiness of the cells and exfoliate the skin. As a result, the pores are unclogged and the skin is smoother and thinner. They are beneficial for some types of acne, including whiteheads, blackheads and mildly inflammatory acne. Some dermatologists in the USA will offer AHA peels as part of their treatment, using glycolic acid.

Beta-hydroxy acid

Otherwise known as salicylic acid, it is keratolytic, which means it will dissolve dead skin cells and thus exfoliate the surface and will help unblock skin pores. Allergic reactions to salicylic acid are quite common. Peels that contain salicylic acid in combination with citric acid and linoleic acid are now available and have been shown to be effective in the treatment of acne (from SkinMed: see Useful addresses).

Microdermabrasion

This is a procedure where a suction tip gently lifts the skin while a fine jet of minute crystals is sprayed across the face, using a hand-held instrument which vacuums the loose dead skin. The skin is left softer, and collagen and elastin formation is stimulated. There is slight stinging during the procedure but side-effects are mild, although they may include redness and mild skin irritation. Microdermabrasion is a very different procedure to dermabrasion (see p. 69), which is not performed on active acne skin. Microdermabrasion can be used to treat superficial acne scars. Unfortunately, this is not available on the NHS. For more on microdermabrasion, see p. 70.

Treatments that affect hormones

The oral contraceptive pill

According to the British Association of Dermatologists, ordinary contraceptive pills have little or no effect on acne. However, prescription of one particular contraceptive pill, Dianette or Diane 35, may be helpful, and anti-androgens that block testosterone are often prescribed alongside, to boost results. The pill works by reducing testosterone production and activation. Side-effects of Dianette are very similar to those of other contraceptive pills and may include weight gain, bleeding and mood changes. In practice it is only effective in clearing acne in 40 per cent of women. It may cause a flare-up of acne in the first month and almost invariably stopping Dianette leads to a flare-up of acne. It is only licensed for women with severe acne who are resistant to conventional forms of acne treatment and should not be given to women with mild acne who want a contraceptive pill. Spironolactone is a potassium-sparing diuretic, with anti-androgenic effects; it has been used in some cases to treat acne, but is not common. You would need to discuss this treatment option with your doctor.

Treatments that decrease oil production

The only topical agent that significantly reduces oil production is Aknicare lotion (Skinmed), where clinical trials have demonstrated up to 70 per cent reduction in oil production.

Anti-androgens in women – Dianette and spironolactone – reduce oil production which is androgen driven.

Oral isotretinoin will decrease oil production, but because of its potency it is used for the treatment of severe acne only.

Intensive light therapy and pulsed dye laser treatment

It has been known for some time that sunlight can help improve acne, at least for a while, but the improvement is short-lived and the potential risk of skin cancer from the ultra-violet rays negates the potential short-term effects. However, the development of light therapy – that is, visible light directly applied to acne skin – is a relatively new treatment. Laser treatment has been around for approximately 20 years, and a new yellow pulsed dye laser treatment – the NLite – has produced some impressive results. According to British dermatologists, this development is the most exciting to arise during the last 30 years in their search for a successful acne treatment.

Recent trials using the NLite laser treatment and led by Professor Tony Chu, consultant dermatologist at Hammersmith Hospital, have recorded a 50 per cent improvement in acne spots for 58 per cent of people, suppressing acne for three months with no side-effects from a single NLite. The NLite pulses a beam of yellow light from a hand-held laser pen onto the skin, where it penetrates the outer layer and, when absorbed by the skin, generates heat and produces chemical changes within the cells. Prof. Chu thinks it is the biological change in the reactivity of skin that is so effective. The skin, believing it is under attack, releases an enormous amount of a chemical called transforming growth factor beta, which down regulates inflammation and increases collagen production. Collagen is required for the repair of the skin and improves acne scarring, at the same time increasing the production of oxygen, which is toxic to bacteria. According to Prof. Chu it is this 'wound-healing cascade' that mysteriously switches off the acne, which he thinks is caused by hypersensitivity to testosterone, and is good news for all those with acne, especially those who feel they are running out of treatment options. The treatment is painless, although there may be a mild warm tingling sensation, and those being treated have to wear an eye mask for the ten-minute sessions, which are given to the whole affected area – face, back or chest.

With antibiotic resistance increasing from 30 per cent in 1992 to 70 per cent in 1997, the use of Roaccutane, a vitamin A derivative, has up until now been considered a last-resort treatment for acne, with its side-effects well documented. While the N-Lite may not be a cure, it does offer significant management and control for this increasing skin disease. You will need to check with your dermatologist whether referral through the NHS is possible for this treatment; private treatment is expensive.

Julie, a 16-year-old teenager from London, had been plagued with acne since the age of ten. Her mother had taken her to the doctor on numerous occasions and treatment had varied from benzoyl peroxide to several courses of antibiotics, but nothing had prevented the acne from recurring and unfortunately scarring.

> I was at my wits' end. With exams, my GCSEs, looming, my spots were worse than ever and I was becoming depressed. One minute I was angry, the next I was crying my eyes out and didn't want to go to school. If the spots weren't bad enough, the scars were starting to show. This time the dermatologist suggested Prof. Chu's NLite treatment or a course of Roaccutane. My mum wasn't keen on me starting that, as I was already depressed, so we went for my first treatment three months ago. The laser didn't hurt at all and I did think I would see some improvement straight away but I didn't, so I was miserable. After about four weeks, though, I noticed a change in my skin: it's improved and the acne is not so red and vicious. I am hoping to go back for a second treatment as we have found out that most improvements need more than one treatment, but it is very expensive. I am quite hopeful – in fact, it's the first time I have felt quite so hopeful in a long time. I haven't started Roaccutane: I think we will wait to see if the second treatment offers more improvement.

There are other forms of light treatment for acne that have been used for the last few years. Blue light treatment was the most usual light treatment people could expect to receive. The blue light, which has none of the UV rays that cause irritation and can damage the skin, could not be used by anyone using medication that increased sensitivity to light. It was mainly used for mild to moderate acne, and was not suitable for severe acne as it could actually make the nodules worse! Furthermore, treatment was not effective for everyone.

But scientists then discovered that a blue and red light combination, where the UV rays were again removed, was the most effective treatment for mild to moderate acne, with significant improvements in inflammatory acne. Although the red light is able to penetrate the tissue more deeply than the blue light and has anti-inflammatory properties, it was the combination of the blue and red light that produced the most dramatic results. The trial, led once again by Prof. Tony Chu, demonstrated that people with acne experienced a 76 per cent reduction of spots after a 12-week period. The blue and red light wavelengths are produced by a light box, used for approximately 15 minutes a day, and visible improvements have been seen within six weeks.

These light boxes, available from Goldstaff by mail order (see Useful addresses under BeautySkin), have the added benefit of being portable, which means they can be used within the comfort of your home. However, it is worthwhile discussing this treatment with your doctor, as it may be possible for you to be referred to a hospital or clinic specializing in this treatment.

Treatment options

Very often it is a combination of treatments which seems to produce the most beneficial effects when treating acne, and determining the type of acne you have will help you to choose the best treatments. As a general rule, retinoids then salicyclic acid, azaelaic acid and benzoyl peroxide are thought to be the most effective for comedones, while benzoyl peroxide, azelaic acid and topical antibiotics are considered the most effective treatments for inflammatory lesions. Retinoids and combination products – topical antibiotics and benzoyl peroxide, for example – are considered effective for both non-inflammatory and inflammatory lesions. However, there is no apparent benefit in combining antibiotic topical treatment with oral antibiotic treatment, and there is the opportunity for the bacteria to become resistant to the treatment.

Mild acne treatment

Mild acne comprises whiteheads, blackheads, small red bumps or a combination of all three. There is no inflammation.

- Begin treatment with a mild over-the-counter topical product: a wash, cream or gel containing benzoyl peroxide or salicylic acid.
- Chart your acne on a weekly basis.
- Consider gentle facials and extractions by a qualified therapist.
- If acne continues, try a low-dose antibiotic product such as clindamycin and benzoyl peroxide.
- If acne still persists, seek a prescription-based antibiotic.
- The alternative may be an oral contraceptive.
- Consider a change in dietary habits, reducing sugar and refined carbohydrates, and if necessary use stress-reducing techniques.
- If acne persists, consult your GP, who will be able to prescribe topical retinoids, antibiotics and antibiotic combinations with benzoyl peroxide or zinc.

Moderate acne treatment

Moderate acne consists of whiteheads, blackheads, raised inflamed red bumps and some pustules and nodules.

- Book an appointment with your doctor, who may prescribe a topical agent containing a retinoid, an antibiotic or a combination product.
- Use a topical wash, cream, lotion or gel containing benzoyl peroxide or azelaic acid, or a topical antibiotic.
- Keep a weekly acne chart.

- It may be necessary to use a combination therapy. Oral antibiotics may be prescribed, along with use of a topical retinoid.
- An oral contraceptive may be prescribed.
- If acne still persists, then you may be referred to a dermatologist for consideration of oral isotretinoin.
- Consider a change in dietary habits, reducing refined carbohydrates and sugar, and if necessary use stress-reducing techniques.

Severe acne treatment

Severe acne causes deep painful cysts and scarring.

- Referral to a consultant dermatologist will be required.
- Surgery or drainage of large cysts may be required. Your doctor or dermatologist will perform this.
- An intralesional injection may be given to help lessen the inflammation and prevent scarring.
- Oral antibiotics may be prescribed.
- Oral contraception may be prescribed.
- Isotretinoin may be prescribed; this is taken for 16–20 weeks and usually only one treatment is required.
- A dermatologist will continue to monitor you during your treatment.

5

Treating acne scars

The advice most doctors would like to give people who suffer from acne is to seek treatment as soon as possible; it is much easier trying to prevent acne from scarring than to find a suitable and successful treatment for scars. Ideally, if your acne is treated early enough, there should be little or no physical scarring. Unfortunately, though, scarring is a fact of life for many people with acne, particularly if treatment started late or wasn't entirely successful.

Why one person suffers from scars and another doesn't is, unfortunately, still not understood, although certain skin colouring and hereditary factors may make some people more predisposed to acne scars than others. There are several treatments which may be offered to help lessen the physical effects of the scar, depending upon the type of scars you have.

What is a scar?

An acne scar is usually a result of severe acne but in some people can occur even with mild acne. Scars occur when there is inflammation from an acne lesion that doesn't heal properly, and tissue damage occurs. White blood cells and anti-inflammatory molecules rush to the inflamed area to fight infection and help heal the damaged tissue. As the skin heals, so scar tissue forms and fills the gaps created in the skin's surface. Although the inflammation will clear, the affected tissue remains in a damaged state, unable to return to normal. The difference between the skin and scar tissue is what makes the scar so visible, and the more inflammation, the more damage to the tissue. The skin can reform itself if the injury is less than 0.5 mm deep or less than a fraction of a millimetre wide; injuries deeper or wider cause scars. Picking or squeezing a spot is not recommended, however tempting it may be, as it can damage the skin tissue so easily.

Typically, acne scars can be raised, level with or lower than the surface skin, and luckily there is much that can be done to help acne-scarred skin. A dermatologist will need to evaluate the type of treatment needed, as different scars require different remedies, so you may be offered more than one. Other factors to consider may include:

- the depth of the scar – a deeper scar is much more likely to require aggressive treatment than a faint scar;
- the type of indentation the scar has left;
- the amount of tissue damage overlying the scar;
- the length of time the scar has been present;
- the degree of improvement expected from the treatment;
- the change in your appearance after treatment.

Types of scars

Some acne lesions will produce red blemishes, known as macules. These macules are also known as pseudo-scars and may change the skin's colour or leave a hyperpigmented mark on the skin, which in time may fade completely. They are considered a post-inflammatory change to the skin rather than an actual scar, where the redness or hyperpigmentation remains as the skin goes through its healing process. This can take anything from 6 to 12 months, providing no more acne occurs in the area. Any remaining change in the skin which leaves a blemish after a year is considered a scar.

Generally there are two types of scars caused by acne: those that cause an increase in tissue formation, and those caused by tissue loss. The scars that increase tissue formation are known as hypertrophic or keloid scars. A hypertrophic scar occurs when the wound heals to become red, raised and itchy, but over time becomes flat and pale. A keloid is very similar, but the scar continues to grow and can become several times larger than the original spot. Both of these scars tend to be found on the chest and back of young people with acne but may occur on the jawline or cheeks. Scars that cause tissue loss are much more common and take many forms, including the so-called icepick, rolling and boxcar scars.

Icepick or 'pock' scares are narrow sharp holes in the skin, generally found on the cheeks and usually narrower than 2 mm. They extend deeply into the dermis, or subcutaneous layer of the skin, and are hard and fibrotic. These types of scars are generally too deep for skin-resurfacing treatments, such as laser treatment, so are usually treated by surgery. Each icepick scar is dealt with individually, usually with a technique known as a punch treatment (see p. 68).

Rolling scars have an undulating appearance and feel about them, looking almost like fingerprints in the skin. They may be soft and can be flattened out easily by lightly stretching the skin or may be held down as they are attached to subcutaneous tissue. Boxcar scars can be very small (looking more like open pores) or large craters but regardless of size they have sharp vertical sides.

Two rare forms of acne, keloid acne and *Acne conglobata*, cause particularly aggressive scarring. Keloid acne stimulates the scar-forming process, sending it into overdrive. Excessive amounts of collagen are produced, and firm raised irregular scar tissue forms. This is commonly found along the jawline, the chest and the back. Very rarely are keloid scars treated by surgery, as they will often form or regrow in response to the surgery itself. If surgery is performed, radiotherapy may be given afterwards to prevent the scar from reforming and growing. The main treatment for keloid scars is the injection of steroids into the scar. This has to be repeated every two months or so until the scar is soft and flat. Even when it is flat, the scar will still leave a visible mark on the skin.

Acne conglobata can leave large pink translucent scars, often referred to as 'tissue paper' scars. They are extremely difficult to treat.

Types of treatment

In order to get rid of or minimize acne scarring, a combination of treatments may be offered.

Topical creams (tretinoin)

A non-surgical form of treatment for very fine acne scarring, topical creams can be applied directly to the scars. They help to stimulate collagen production in the skin and may also be applied to depressed scars before another treatment is used.

Chemical peels

Chemical peels involve a procedure where acid is applied to the skin in order to accelerate the removal of old dead cells from the skin surface. This then promotes new cell growth. There are three types of peels, superficial, medium and deep. All three require pre-treatment products to be used at home before the peel is applied. The peels can be used on specific areas, such as around the eyes or mouth, as well as over the face and neck. Peels can take anything from a few minutes to over 30 minutes.

Superficial peels

Superficial peels remove the top layer of skin cells, or epidermis, and have to be performed by either a qualified beauty therapist or a dermatologist. A combination of alpha-hydroxy acids (AHAs) and beta-hydroxy acids (BHAs), glycolic acid, lactic acid, salicylic acid and maleic acid are used. Treatment takes only a few minutes, and afterwards the skin may look pink and feel tight for a couple of hours. Treatment for at least six weeks may be required before any results are visible.

Medium peels

Medium peels penetrate the skin deeper, removing the skin cells from the epidermis and the upper dermis (the middle layer of skin), and have to be performed by a dermatologist. Trichloroacetic acid (TCA) is normally used in these peels, and is sometimes combined with glycolic acid. The peel remains on the skin for a few minutes and is then neutralized. A burning or stinging sensation may be felt during and after treatment, and skin can be very red or even go brown afterwards. Although, this will settle down it can take up to six weeks for the skin to go back to normal after this peel. Treatment may have to be repeated every 6–12 months to sustain results.

Deep peels

Deep peels penetrate the dermis, and are only performed by a dermatologist or surgeon. Phenol is the main ingredient, and a local anaesthetic may be given before the procedure takes place. The results can be dramatic. The peel is applied to the face and left for approximately 30 minutes. During this time the person feels as if his or her face is 'freezing'. After treatment painkillers may be required, and there may also be peeling and redness. The skin needs to be protected from the sun and UVA rays after treatment, and the dermatologist will offer support and post-treatment information. This type of peel is a one-off treatment, unlike the other two chemical peels.

Punch techniques

These are treatments most suited to icepick scars. There are three types of punch techniques, but they all use an instrument called a punch biopsy tool, which looks similar to a pastry cutter. The methods used are known as:

- punch excision, where the scar is removed under local anaesthetic by the punch tool and the wound is left to close and heal;

- punch elevation, where the walls of the scar are left intact and just the base of the scar is cut, then lifted to the surrounding level of the skin;
- punch replacement, where the scar is removed by the punch biopsy tool and the area is filled by skin grafting, usually with skin from behind the back of the person's ear.

Skin fillers

These are another treatment for acne scars. They can be used on their own or in combination with other scar treatments. Fillers literally plump up, or fill out, the skin where the scar has caused it to sink. They are also used when the sunken scar has been forced upwards, through nearby skin being overstretched. Fillers are composed of collagen, the person's own fat, and polymer implants, which are injected directly into the scar. Although they may only work as a short-term method (6–12 months) they can be repeated, and this treatment may improve some scars by up to 50 per cent.

In some cases, cosmetic surgeons may use hyaluronic acid, a natural material for acne scars. This acid helps to glue the skin cells together, and is considered an alternative skin filler.

Dermabrasion

Dermabrasion removes the surface of the skin, so shallow and nodular scars become less obvious. There are two types of dermabrasion, one that requires a motorized tool known as a dermatome, and another which uses a fine wire brush. The dermatome has a spinning metal head, similar to an electric razor. This treatment promotes healing of the skin, encouraging and stimulating collagen, which plumps up the sunken areas of scarring, and the results are usually long-lasting. The procedure can take up to an hour, and is performed under local anaesthetic by a surgeon or dermatologist. Bear in mind it may take several weeks before the scabs heal and the redness of the skin has subsided. The treatment can only be used on acne skin that is no longer active, otherwise infection, inflammation and possible scarring may occur. Dermabrasion should not be confused with microdermabrasion.

Microdermabrasion

Microdermabrasion involves a fine jet of minute crystals being sprayed across the person's face, using a hand-held instrument which vacuums up the loose dead skin. The flow of the crystals and the vacuum are pressurized according to skin type and the desired result. This treatment is suitable for shallow acne scars, and is often used before laser or pulsed light treatment is given, to improve the penetration of the light through the skin.

Microdermabrasion stimulates collagen growth and realigns the skin's cells in the epidermis, which causes the skin to thicken. After treatment the skin may be red for a few days. There are several different microdermabrasion treatments available; they vary in intensity, and treatment may be performed by a qualified beauty therapist or a surgeon, depending upon the strength of the treatment involved.

Laser treatments

Laser treatments are most suited to shallow scars, and are either ablative or non-ablative. Ablative treatment or laser resurfacing removes the top layer of the skin; it literally burns off or vaporizes the skin, and is generally more precise than mechanical abrasion. It has been a popular treatment but is falling out of favour due to the long down time after treatment and the fact that it can cause the skin to become red or darker depending on your skin type. Non-ablative laser or subsurfacing treatment works on skin underneath the top layer, stimulating new collagen production without injury to the skin. It is much slower than ablative laser but there is no downtime and no obvious visible effect on the skin following treatment.

After ablative laser skin resurfacing treatment, the skin may remain red for a considerable time, in some cases for up to six months, and it is necessary to protect the skin from the sun for at least a year after treatment. The most commonly used lasers for acne include

- carbon dioxide (CO_2) laser
- erbium YAG (ErYAG) laser
- long-pulsed erbium (YAG) laser – pulsed, yellow light.

Subcision

Sometimes a procedure known as a subcision may be used to treat tethered rolling acne scars. It involves inserting a specialized sterile needle with a cutting blade at the tip into the base of the scar. The fibrous strands of scar tissue are cut, encouraging collagen fibres to fill the depressed area of the scar and raising the sunken skin to the surface. Following subcision, the skin is often swollen for three to four days and there can be a lot of deep bruising which may last two weeks or so.

Dermaroller

The Dermaroller was developed in Germany and is not widely used, but it is a very effective method of treating acne scars. It is based on the principle of needling – if you insert a hypodermic needle into the skin, it will not leave a permanent mark as it is too small but will generate considerable new collagen production. The Dermaroller is a small metal wheel which is studded with over 100 1.5mm needles. This is rolled up and down the scarred area leaving thousands of punctures which generate lots of new collagen production. The skin is very red for up to four days after treatment but soon settles with no long-term problems.

Fraxel laser

The Fraxel laser is a CO_2 laser where the laser beam is split into thousands of tiny beamlets. It works on the same principle as the Dermaroller, producing thousands of tiny injuries to the skin, which in turn leads to new collagen production. Down time can be several days.

Trichloracetic acid (TCA) CROSS technique

CROSS stands for cross-sectional reconstruction of skin scars. It is a technique developed in Korea and involves the careful application of 100 per cent TCA, using a sharpened orange stick, to the base of boxcar scars. This causes an injury to the skin and considerable, very local, production of collagen. It is one of the few methods that can effectively treat boxcar scars.

Preventing scarring

There are certain things you can do to help to prevent scarring from occurring.

1 Seek treatment soon. Early treatment is the best preventative against permanent scars, or those that are difficult to treat. The longer acne is tolerated before treatment, the higher the likelihood of scarring.
2 Wash your face daily in antibacterial soap or solutions.
3 Try not to pick your spots, tempting though it may be. You are more likely to damage the skin around the spot, creating scar tissue and inflammation. If you do need to squeeze a spot then apply heat to the area first to open the pore, clean with an alcohol-based cleanser and apply pressure on either side of the spot. Once the pus or blackhead has been expressed, stop squeezing – if you see blood you have damaged the lower part of the skin and could be left with a scar!
4 Protect your skin from the sun – use factor 15+ sunscreen for daily use, especially on the face, and avoid getting sunburnt.

5 Use non-comedogenic cosmetics, face and hair products.
6 Consider taking essential fatty acid supplements (EFAs). These have anti-inflammatory effects on the skin, as they are converted into prostaglandin, a hormone-like substance. The body cannot make EFAs; they have to be found in your diet. Gamma linoleic acid is particularly useful and is present in evening primrose oil and star fruit oil. Omega 3 fatty acids also seem to be beneficial; they decrease systemic inflammation, often found in those with acne. Omega 3 can be found in flaxseed oil, salmon, mackerel and other oily fish.
7 Exfoliate your skin regularly using alpha-hydroxy acids. These increase the rate of cell production, decrease the stickiness of the cells and exfoliate the skin. The dead layer of skin is made thinner and smoother, and the opening of the pore is less likely to be blocked. Glycolic acid is the most popular type of peel.

6

Complementary therapies

Although many people with acne follow the conventional treatment route for their acne, others prefer the more 'natural' form of treatment and find that alternative and complementary medicine suits them better. Some choose to combine both conventional and alternative treatments. Doctors more readily accept some than others, and they may even be able to offer referrals on the NHS for certain complementary treatments, such as Homoeopathy.

Many complementary therapies can be used to improve the quality of life for the person with acne. Some use stress-relaxing techniques, and many suggest simple lifestyle changes, including exercise or diet. It can be difficult to know which ones to consider; however, the most popular types of alternative therapy used to treat acne include Homoeopathy, Western and Chinese herbs, and Ayurvedic medicine. Before you embark upon an alternative method of treatment for your acne, it may be worthwhile considering the following:

- Most alternative therapies are not funded by the NHS, so you may have to pay for your treatments.
- Use a qualified therapist. He or she should be registered, and a member of the relevant organization for the therapy in question – for example, a herbalist from the National Institute of Medical Herbalists, or a Homoeopath from the British Homoeopathic Association.
- Ask your therapist when he or she would expect to see results from the treatment. How long is treatment anticipated to take, and what is required from you to enable the therapy to be most effective?

- What works for one individual may not work for another (although the same can also be said for conventional medicine).
- If you are using conventional treatment, inform your doctor or dermatologist that you are thinking of using 'alternative' treatment as well.
- Your complementary therapist should ask you about any medication you are taking.
- Check your medication will not react with the therapy.
- It is always better to seek qualified advice than to self-treat.

Homoeopathy

Homoeopathy is one of the most popular forms of complementary medicine, and is based on the idea of 'treating like with like'. Homoeopaths prescribe very small doses of substances which, when taken by a healthy person, can cause symptoms similar to those of which the person complains. Homoeopathy is also a holistic treatment – homoeopaths don't treat diseases, they treat people. This means that there is no one homoeopathic treatment for acne; different homoeopathic medicines are used for different types of people with different types of acne, which is very often why one person's prescription will differ from another person's, even though they both have acne.

Dr Peter Fisher, MRCP, FFHom, clinical director at the Royal London Homoeopathic Hospital (RLHH), deals with people who have acne and other skin conditions and disorders. He believes that 'between 50 and 65 per cent of patients attending NHS homoeopathic hospitals report at least moderate improvement of their acne, but unfortunately homoeopathy will not help with scarring left behind by acne'.

According to Dr Fisher, among the homoeopathic medicines most commonly prescribed for acne are sulphur and silica.

Acne, which responds to silica, is characterized by pustules, which never seem to discharge: they sit under the skin for weeks without discharging, often forming cysts. The type of person for whom silica would be prescribed is usually chilly, feeling the cold excessively. She often has weak, ridged nails, and her hands and feet are cold yet clammy. She may complain of feeling tired yet may be stubborn and 'niggly'. In contrast, the type of person who is likely to respond to sulphur is extrovert and untidy. She tends to be 'hot-blooded', needing fewer clothes than most people, and her acne spots often itch or burn.

Pulsatilla is another remedy which may be helpful in acne, particularly (but not only) in women who get crops of spots in the premenstrual period. The type of person who responds to pulsatilla is said to be mild-tempered and indecisive, often weepy but quickly cheered up by a few reassuring words. Strangely, although 'pulsatilla types' tend to feel the cold, they like fresh air and hate stuffy atmospheres.

This is by no means a comprehensive account of the homoeopathic treatment of acne, but if one of these 'pictures' seems to chime with you, it is worth trying homoeopathic treatment. You can buy the homoeopathic medicines mentioned above in many high street pharmacies (including Boots) and health food shops. You should start with the 6 c strength (the strength usually stocked by chemists), and take two pills twice a day.

Homoeopathy is very safe – if it does no good, it will not do any harm. But sometimes the right homoeopathic medicine causes an 'aggravation' at first. This means that it gets worse before it gets better, and is a good sign. But if you do get such an aggravation, you should stop the treatment until it has completely settled down, and then start again. You may get an aggravation the second time round, but it will be less severe. Because homoeopathy works by stimulating the body's own healing processes, the duration of treatment is proportionate to the length of time you have had acne: if it started recently, the response should be quite quick, but if you have had it several years you may need six months or more of treatment. However, the effect is long-term: you do not need to keep taking the medicine indefinitely, although you may need an occasional 'top-up'. There are many other possible homoeopathic treatments for acne apart from those mentioned above, so it may well be worth consulting a practitioner.

You can get a list of qualified homoeopathic doctors from the British Homeopathic Association (see Useful addresses).

Homoeopathy is available on the NHS, and there are homoeopathic hospitals in London, Glasgow, Bristol and Liverpool. You need a letter of referral from your GP to be seen on the NHS.

Herbal medicine

Herbs have been used as drugs or in drugs for centuries, and according to the National Institute of Medical Herbalists, today's Western herbalists 'combine historical knowledge with the latest scientific research'. Herbalists often prescribe anti-inflammatory and antibacterial herbs for acne: calendula, witch hazel, tea tree oil, German chamomile, liquorice root, flaxseed and flaxseed oil are all good examples. They work on the basis of reducing the amount of *P. acnes* bacteria, and reducing further secondary infection. Diuretics, hormone normalizers and antimicrobial herbs are used to help, both topically and internally, supporting the endocrine system.

Trudy Norris, of the National Institute of Medical Herbalists, suggests herbs can be very beneficial for acne.

Herbalists take an individual approach, assessing, treating and reviewing any prescription regularly. Following assessment a herbalist will be able to give you an idea of what they are looking for as an outcome, for example typical timescales. Treatment will vary depending upon how long and what type of acne someone has.

As with any condition, individual influences are identified and addressed. For example, in the case of a woman with menstrual-related acne, a prescription might include herbs with anti-inflammatory, antiseptic and immune-enhancing properties, together with a regulatory effect on the endocrine system.

Herbs may also be used to influence the lymphatic system. It would be unusual for herbal treatment to be too long, and generally I would look for a positive change with the first prescription. Herbs are gentle but effective, with improvements sustained, especially if recommended lifestyle changes have been adhered to. These lifestyle changes include making adjustments and improvements to diet, managing stress and taking regular exercise. Increasing fluid intake will also generally have a positive effect on acne.

Herbs that are used to treat chronic skin complaints are safe, with rare side-effects, and are well tolerated. They can be used safely under qualified guidance by all age groups.

Of course, some people will often try and self-diagnose. The following are the most popular herbs used when self-diagnosing:

- Amarant: use to make a tea from the seeds, and as a face wash.
- Basil: make a tea from the leaves, leave to cool, and apply to the acne with clean cotton wool.
- Burdock: the herb burdock (*Arctium lappa*) is considered the most important herb for treating all forms of skin problems, including acne. Tea is made from the root and applied cool, as a body wash.
- Calendula: this is found in tinctures, lotions and creams, or made as a tea and applied as a wash.
- Herbal teas: there are several other herbs suitable for acne that can be made into a tea, to be drunk or used as a wash. They include aloe, chickweed, dandelion, red clover, echinacea, ginseng and valerian.

Ayurvedic medicine

An ancient healthcare system native to the Indian subcontinent, Ayurvedic medicine is the oldest known form of medicine. It is the system of medicine practised today in India, Sri Lanka and Pakistan. The term 'Ayurveda' is taken from the Sanskrit words *ayus*, meaning life or lifespan, and *veda*, meaning knowledge. Ayurvedic medicine uses detoxification, diet, herbs and exercise to improve health and mental and emotional well-being.

Just as everyone has a unique thumbprint, according to Ayurvedic beliefs each person has a distinct pattern of energy – a specific combination of physical, mental and emotional characteristics. It is also believed that there are three basic energy types, called *doshas*, present in every person, and these determine the basic body type:

- *vata* – energy that regulates body functions associated with blood circulation;
- *pitta* – energy that governs the body's metabolic systems, including digestion and body temperature;
- *kapha* – energy that controls growth in the body. It supplies water to all parts of the body, moisturizes the skin and maintains the immune system.

Many factors, including stress, diet, lifestyle, the environment and hormones, are thought to disturb the *dosha* balance, and these disturbances are expressed as disease in the body, acne being a skin disease. Ayurvedic practitioners prescribe treatments, usually through diet and herbs, yoga and meditation to rebalance the *doshas*.

Traditional Chinese Medicine

Traditional Chinese Medicine, or TCM, is a 5,000-year-old Chinese medicine system with a holistic approach. It combines acupuncture, Chinese herbs, dietary therapy, exercises in breathing and movement, such as Tai Chi, and, in some cases, massage. It is still widely practised in the East, and is gaining popularity here in the West.

TCM is based on the concept of yin and yang, meridians or pathways of energy that must be balanced for energy – or chi, the life force – to flow through them. When there is an imbalance, there is illness or disease. The Chinese believe that acne is linked to inefficient and incomplete digestion, and Chinese medicine prescribes herbs for clearing and cleansing the digestive system.

According to Don Mei, a spokesman for the AcuMedic clinic, the oldest and largest Chinese clinical organization outside Asia,

> Acne can be treated successfully with Chinese medicine, and is often used in conjunction with Western medical care. According to Chinese medicine, all skin disorders are the result of an imbalance in the body, which can be triggered by many different factors, such as diet, stress and hormonal imbalance. The imbalances usually associated with acne are damp heat from the stomach and intestines, blood stasis (poor blood flow) and excessive heat in the lungs. Every individual is different and the cause of acne can be a combination of these factors. A properly qualified Chinese medical doctor will talk to the individual, perform a pulse and tongue diagnosis, and assess any particular imbalances.
>
> Chinese herbal medicines in the form of a hot drink, herbal skin lotions and sometimes acupuncture are used to rebalance the body, and therefore remove the root cause of the acne. The course of treatment is normally over a few weeks.

Emma Farrent, a practitioner of Chinese herbal medicine, looks to find a pattern when treating an acne client. She says,

> I often see patients after they have had unsuccessful results from conventional treatment for acne. I treat the individual and have been relatively successful, especially with women who have acne. Recently I treated a woman in her forties who had a flare-up of acne. Within seven weeks her skin had responded well to the treatment, and after six months she stopped treatment, as it was no longer needed. Very often the red and purplish colour of the skin is what we refer to as blood stagnation, and typical of acne in older people. Teenage acne is usually more to do with heat and an imbalance in the patient's yin and yang. It is generally easier to treat than adult acne.

Aloe vera

This is a plant with several properties that promote healing and restoring of the skin, especially from infections, burns and scars. The plant has been used for its therapeutic properties for over 4,000 years. You can buy aloe vera products from a health food shop or supermarket; they include juice, gel, lotion and cream. The cream is thought to help reduce the inflammation and redness associated with acne. Aloe vera soaps are kinder to the skin than other soaps and can be used, along with aloe vera shampoo, considered non-comedogenic, for acne skin.

If your skin is scarred from acne, using aloe vera juice morning and night, for as long as necessary (perhaps six months or longer), is thought to help improve the skin's complexion and the colour of the scar itself. If you do have a plant at home then the pulp of the leaf is a good skin cleaner. It can be rubbed directly onto the skin and any dirt, make-up or dead skin cells removed with cotton wool.

Traditional or folk remedies

There are many traditional folk remedies for treating skin conditions. There is no scientific evidence to support their claims, but a selection of those considered suitable for acne include:

- Apple cider vinegar or lemon juice: the lemon juice or apple cider vinegar is applied to clean skin. It is thought the acid in these ingredients helps keep the skin clear, as well as balancing the acidity or alkalinity of your skin.
- Honey and cinnamon: these ingredients are mixed together into a paste and spread over acne skin.
- Toothpaste: thought to help dry up spots, toothpaste is applied to the spots at night and washed off in the morning.
- Fruit: watermelon pulp, strawberry juice and even a mashed papaya, spread over your skin, are some of the fruits recommended to help treat your acne.
- Mint: using a few crushed mint leaves and the extracted mint juice, place the leaves into a muslin cloth and apply directly to the scars.
- Neem: this is a fast-growing tree, native to India. The oil,

leaves and bark contain effective and soothing ingredients, very useful for acne skin. It also helps keeps the skin's elasticity and has antifungal, antibacterial, antiviral and anti-inflammatory effects. Neem oil is used in soaps, creams, shampoos and balms, and Neem can be bought in most health food shops. It is very often used in Ayurvedic treatments.

Exercise

According to researchers from Bath University, people suffering from acne tend to stay away from exercise, through shyness or 'dermatological social anxiety'. Yet exercise and sport can actually help to improve the skin and well-being. On a physical level, exercise boosts oxygen to the cells and increases blood flow to the skin, so improving skin health. It also aids the digestive system, helping to expel toxins from the body. Research has shown that regular exercise not only strengthens the immune system, but also helps to reduce stress and rebalances hormones, both of which are major contributors to acne.

On a psychological level, exercise makes you feel better. It improves the health of your body and your mind through the production of endorphins, creating the 'feel-good factor', which improves your mood and self-confidence. As well as looking better, you feel good too.

Exercise also helps to promote sleep, and sleep is considered important in helping to reduce stress and lessen the effects of acne. Recent studies have revealed that moderate to vigorous exercise, three to four times a week, for at least 20–30 minutes, helps to promote good-quality sleep. Just make sure you don't exercise vigorously late in the evening, or you'll be too energized to sleep!

Exercise needs to include cardiovascular activity, to increase the heart rate, and cycling, jogging, running, swimming, squash and tennis are all activities that will help do this. The government guidelines are for 20–30 minutes' exercise five times a week, but don't feel that you can't do any more than this. The benefits of exercise really do improve the quality of your life. One of the best ways to ensure you stick to regular exercise is to do it with someone else, on a sociable level, and this is more encouraging too. Even brisk walking is beneficial, and relatively inexpensive, although it is worthwhile investing in the appropriate footwear for your preferred activity.

For those suffering from acne, make sure the clothes you wear for exercise don't cause friction or rub against the skin. Natural fibres are usually best, and sportswear manufacturers tend to produce clothing that removes sweat from the skin. Helmets are generally the worst culprits for causing spots, so remove them as soon as you have finished your activity, and try to shower as soon as possible after exercise, particularly if you have become hot and sweaty, as this will help reduce bacteria from the skin's surface. It is also best to remove make-up before exercise: if you do get hot and sweaty you can plug the pores with foundation or make-up. Stay hydrated by drinking water before, during and after exercise, and if necessary use a sunscreen when you are going to be exercising outside.

Yoga and Tai Chi

Both of these forms of exercise have been practised for thousands of years. Promoting a sense of well-being, they combine stretching exercises with breath control and meditation. Excessive stress affects the production of the stress hormones, including cortisol, and both yoga and Tai Chi are thought to help reduce stress, promoting physical, mental and emotional benefits. Classes are the best way to learn these exercises, and are usually available locally.

7

The relationship between stress and acne

Stress can have such a negative effect on your body and in particular affects your skin health. Among other effects, it is known to accelerate the ageing process of the skin and make it look dull and lifeless. It weakens the skin's barrier and eventually decreases its ability to protect against harmful irritants, which in the long run can lead to various skin disorders such as eczema, rashes and acne. The more stressed you are, the more likely you are to have an outbreak, especially if you are prone to acne.

The true psychological and physical effects of stress are only just being realized, and the good news is that responding appropriately to stress helps to lower its impact. It has only been recently that doctors have realized that stress really does make acne worse, and many medical professionals now recognize that reducing tension, anxiety and worry will help to reduce the effects of stress and may help to control acne flare-ups. Your doctor may therefore suggest some lifestyle changes in the hope that they will help lower stress levels. These may include some simple changes to diet, suggested forms of exercise, stopping smoking and reducing alcohol intake; they may also include relaxation techniques such as meditation, yoga or even relaxation classes to help lower stress levels and mitigate acne.

Overactive immune system and stress

The immune system can play a significant role in causing and worsening inflammatory acne. Stimulated by stress, the immune system reacts in an excessive, aggressive manner. It attacks the

P. acnes bacterium in the hair follicles with great enthusiasm, as if it were life-threatening, and as a result lays down fibrous scar tissue around the infection, inflammation or red tender acne lesion. This scar tissue then pulls down on the hair follicle, resulting in a depressed or sunken scar on the skin. Controlling and reducing stress is the only method which can help stop the immune system from reacting naturally to the stimulation of the stress hormones.

Understanding your stress triggers

We live in stressful times: modern daily living is fast and furious, and many people feel under pressure. Each individual's reaction to stress is different, however. For some, stress is nothing more than a feeling of apprehension or 'butterflies' in the stomach, while many others may experience more dramatic or emotional feelings. Everyday occurrences such as traffic jams, waiting in queues or being late for school or work may put us under stress. Other events such as exams, relationship problems and financial worries can exacerbate stress levels, leaving us feeling out of control.

Once you have identified what makes you stressed you can make some positive changes to help you lower your stress levels.

Robert, 19, knows only too well the misery stress can bring.

Although I had acne at 14 it didn't affect me too much, but when I started to prepare for my GCSEs I noticed my acne changed. Now I seemed to wake up with huge red pus-filled inflamed spots. It was awful. The more anxious I got over the looming exams, the worse they got, and then I started becoming anxious over my spots. It was terrible – nothing seemed to help them. The doctor told me I was stressed but I didn't know what to do about it. My mum said they would go once my exams were over and they did, but it took about two to three months. By the time I came to take my A levels I knew what to expect, and sure enough it happened again. Only this time it wasn't quite so bad.

I carried on playing football twice a week and I think this helped me deal with the stress better. I'm just hoping they don't come back during exam time at university.

Dermatologists acknowledge that many people feel their acne is worse when they are under pressure. Identifying and understanding your own individual stress triggers is important to help you take control and manage your stress, and it is well worth learning new techniques or strategies to help you control or change the way you react to events.

Common stress signs

It's all very well knowing you have to reduce your stress and identifying what your stress triggers are, but of course you need to know just how stress manifests itself. There are both mental and physical symptoms of stress, and the most common mental symptoms include

- tension
- irritability
- inability to concentrate
- problems sleeping
- feeling fatigued all the time
- no energy.

Physical symptoms include

- a pounding heart
- sweaty palms
- a dry mouth
- shaking uncontrollably
- difficulty breathing
- an upset stomach
- butterflies in the stomach
- frequent urination.

Reducing stress

There are several steps you can take to help yourself combat the negative effects of stress. Remember that you will need to continue appropriate treatment for your acne at the same time as lowering your stress levels. Feeling in control of your acne rather than your acne being in control of you will also help. There are some simple steps to help reduce stress which you can try, but if you really feel stressed, or your acne is seriously affecting your life, then make sure you go and see your doctor and discuss this.

It's not just people with acne who get stressed, of course; we all do to some degree or another. The methods we choose to adopt to deal with stress vary, and it's worth trying a few simple ones to see which work for you. Everyone can benefit from relaxation techniques, which vary from yoga and Tai Chi classes through to meditation, visualization and autogenic training. If attending a class is difficult, relaxation CDs are also available and you can use them at home to help you unwind, especially at the end of the day – but please don't use them while driving or in the car.

Simple methods, such as a soak in a warm bath, reading or having a massage, will all help you to relax, although you may find a massage is not suitable if the skin on your chest and back is covered with acne lesions. Deep breathing, releasing muscle tension or just taking time out can all help.

Finding time for exercise is especially beneficial. Not only does it reduce stress, but also it also makes you feel better and promotes your overall health and well-being. Try a new sport or an exercise class to get the best from your exercise, or join the craze and take up dancing.

Make sure you get enough sleep; anxiety and tension often adversely affect sleep and this plays havoc with your skin and your health. Lack of sleep raises your cortisol levels and floods your bloodstream with hormones that induce acne.

Make sure you eat a healthy diet; stress can often cause weight gain as it increases the fat around your middle, which will in time have adverse effects on your health. The stress hormones increase the natural desire to eat, so we consume more, and after a period of excess stress fat is added as an extra layer below the abdominal muscle.

Unhealthy eating depletes the necessary vitamins and minerals required to keep your body functioning properly. This can in turn affect your mood, sleeping patterns, metabolism and body temperature, and may even lead to depression. A study in America conclusively proved that acne among students was significantly worse during their exams, and their diets tended to be much more unhealthy during the run-up to the exam period, contributing considerably to their acne flare-ups – another study suggesting that diet does have an influence on acne. And don't forget drinking. Alcohol can increase your weight and won't help you deal with stress in the long term.

Learning to prioritize and manage time also helps reduce stress. All too often the pressures of trying to do too much leave you feeling unable to cope. Simple time management strategies can help reclaim some control over your life and improve your self-confidence – writing lists, for example, and separating work from home duties while planning for the immediate, short-term and long-term future can also help people feel better able to cope.

Stress doesn't vanish overnight, but it can be reduced with a little help. It may mean you have to try new methods and ways, just as you may have had to with your acne treatment, but it will make a difference eventually.

Easy stress busters

- Get a hobby. It may be creative, sporting, physical or even educational – it doesn't matter what you choose, just have a go. Local education centres run hundreds of classes if you really don't know where to start.

- Get outside. A daily walk for 20 to 30 minutes in the fresh air really does make you feel better.
- Find some friends and have a laugh. The power of laughter is enormous and helps to rid you of stress.
- Write a journal. Actually recording your stress and relating it to your acne outbreak may make you more aware of what your stress triggers are.

Sleep

There is no doubt about it, sleep plays a very important role in your skin's health. A good night's sleep helps to restore the body, encouraging it to build a strong immune system, a vital ingredient in the fight against acne. Although it won't mean your skin will not suffer from acne, it does mean your acne lesions will clear more quickly, as the infection is destroyed.

During your sleep the skin cells are nourished and regenerated, so that your body literally restores itself while you are sleeping. The body absorbs free radicals from environmental factors including diet, exercise, stress, pollution, caffeine, smoking and alcohol during the day, and it is at night and during sleep that the body is able to detoxify. However, if sleep patterns are disturbed or shortened, hormone levels are affected and your body is unable to restore itself back to its equilibrium, resulting in excess sebum being produced and more acne lesions, along with moodiness, lack of concentration and low energy levels.

Lack of sleep can also raise stress and anxiety levels, making it more difficult for you to deal with the daily stresses you normally encounter. Once your stress levels are raised your hormone levels are affected, as are sebum production and blocked pores – the vicious circle of acne begins again.

It's not just your sleep you have to think about when going to bed, but your clothing and bedlinen too. If your clothes are too tight and rub against your skin, they may irritate it and spots will appear. Likewise, your bedlinen should be clean, particularly your pillowcases if you have acne on your face. Lying with your skin against the linen can cause irritation; a clean pillowcase every night will help to minimize the spread of bacteria and infection. It might also be worthwhile sleeping on anti-dust-mite linen, mattresses and pillows, so no other skin irritants can affect you.

Sleeping soundly

Teenagers like to stay up late and get up late, which is all very well in the holidays but more difficult when they are at school or college, and particularly during exam periods. It might be hard work, but getting your teenager to accept a regular sleeping pattern of six to eight hours will benefit his or her skin. It might be difficult at first, but the results will literally show for themselves on the skin. Establishing a regular sleeping pattern is the key for teenagers and adults with acne, and there are a variety of ways you can help yourself, or your teenager, to make it easier and simpler to get a good night's sleep.

Sleep tips

1 Establish a routine, and go to bed at the same time most evenings. This helps your body get used to a regular sleep pattern.
2 Prepare for bed. Your wind-down period should include cleaning your face; you probably have an established acne cleansing routine at the end of the day, which you follow before bedtime.
3 Lie on your back. This helps to keep your face off the bedlinen and is less irritating to your skin.
4 No eating or drinking too late. Eating a late meal will mean

you feel full and heavy. Night time is the period of restoration for the body: letting it recover without adding to its workload is beneficial to optimizing your health.

5 Avoid caffeine in chocolate, tea, coffee or fizzy drinks before bedtime, and dairy too. It's an old wives' tale that a milky drink induces sleep, and if you do drink alcohol at night time make sure you drink plenty of water to stop yourself becoming dehydrated. The only trouble is, you might then end up having to get up at night to go to the toilet, disturbing your sleep!

6 Take the television out of the bedroom. Overstimulating the mind before bedtime can keep you awake.

7 Take exercise in the day, preferably in the fresh air for at least 30 minutes, each and every day. But don't exercise too late at night either, as this can also keep you awake.

8 You need to make sure your bedroom is well ventilated and not too hot.

9 Make sure your bed is comfortable. It might sound silly, but an uncomfortable bed will make relaxing and sleeping soundly difficult, no matter how tired you are.

10 If you are stressed then make sure you try and relax before you get to bed. Try yoga or mediation or deep breathing. Even listening to a relaxation tape will help to soothe your mind.

11 If you take a nap in the day then keep it short – about 45 minutes is enough.

12 Keep your room dark. Early morning light flooding in through the windows will disturb your sleep.

13 Try not to think. This can be really difficult, especially if you have some work or relationship problem or are studying for exams. Have a pen and notepad at the side of your bed to write down anything that is troubling you; that way you can let it go.

14 Lavender oil is good for relaxation. Put a few drops on your

pillow or burn some in your bedroom before you go to bed. Make sure you blow the candle out before you sleep, though.

15 Take out of your room any work-related objects, or cover them over if you can't do this. Leave the work area alone before bedtime and switch off all electrical appliances at the socket.

16 Take a warm bath – not too hot, or the increase in body temperature will keep you awake.

17 If you really aren't sleepy, get up and read for a little while. Then try again.

18 Don't smoke at night, particularly before bedtime, as nicotine is a stimulant.

19 Try drinking chamomile tea before bedtime.

20 Get up at the same time every morning, even if you feel tired.

8

Acne and diet

For years dermatologists were adamant that diet did not influence or affect acne. However, recent scientific research suggests the link between diet and acne does exist, particularly in a Western diet. The *American Journal of Clinical Nutrition* published a report from researchers who believe it isn't the particular food you eat, like pizza or chocolate, that triggers acne, but the typical Western diet itself.

Research by Australian scientists at the RMIT University and Royal Melbourne Hospital Department of Dermatology, who discovered the link between diet and acne, found it related directly to the changes in glucose and insulin levels brought about by certain foods which affected and influenced skin changes. They discovered that foods with a high glycaemic index, typical of those consumed in a Western diet, caused a sharp rise in glucose and insulin levels, and were more likely to influence the development and severity of acne. Protein and low glycaemic carbohydrates were seen to lessen the effects of acne, and the study has prompted more research.

Although there is no official advice about diet and acne yet, healthy eating will always certainly improve your health. The general guidelines of eating a minimum of five portions of fruit and vegetables a day, drinking plenty of water and reducing foods high in saturated fat and salt are recommended for everyone, not just for those with acne. Eating healthily will help to promote good skin, so it has to be beneficial to make some simple dietary changes to help bring about some positive results. And while your diet may not cause your acne, if you are predisposed to acne your diet is much more likely to aggravate or trigger it.

Foods that may trigger acne

Certain foods are thought to be more acne-inducing than others.

Simple carbohydrates

These foods form the basis of much of the Western diet and are considered major contributors to the growing obesity problem. Pizza bases, white bread, refined flour, cakes, pastries, white rice and pasta are all part of many Westerners' staple diet. High in refined carbohydrates, such foods raise the blood sugar rapidly, releasing glucose for energy, and are rated as high glycaemic foods. The glycaemic index (GI) measures the rate or speed at which individual foods are digested, and this depends upon the amount of carbohydrates, protein, fats and fibre they contain. It is the carbohydrate component which affects blood sugar levels, with low GI foods raising blood sugar levels slowly and high GI foods raising blood sugar levels rapidly.

Rapid rises and falls in blood sugar levels affect energy and cause cravings, which can lead to overeating and weight gain. High GI foods increase levels of insulin, and an insulin-like growth factor, IGF-1, increases the production of the male hormone testosterone. This in turn stimulates the overproduction of sebum, inflammation and acne.

Eating mostly low GI foods will ensure you are left feeling full and will help to control surges in blood sugar, reducing possible acne lesions. Foods to eat include whole grains, lentils, fruit, brown rice, potatoes and root vegetables, while foods to avoid include refined and processed foods, fried foods, biscuits, cakes, pastries and fizzy drinks.

Milk

Milk is thought to affect and aggravate acne, particularly in women, because of the natural and synthetic hormones it contains. The hormones naturally produced by the cow include DHT, a by-product of testosterone, found naturally in teenagers, and the IGF-1 hormone. Saturated fats common in dairy products are also thought to initiate acne, and are linked to several other health conditions including hardening of the arteries, heart disease, stroke, diabetes and certain cancers. These fats are also thought to increase bacteria, a precursor to acne.

Although there is still little scientific evidence, some nutritionists suggest milk and dairy products should be removed from the diet if you have or are prone to acne, a theory that is supported by an American dermatologist, Nicholas Perricone.

Meat

Red meat is known to contain artificial hormones and steroids, and there is concern that these may upset the natural hormonal balance within the body. An acidic food, meat can sometimes be difficult to digest and creates toxins, a by-product of acid-forming food, which can often end up for prolonged periods in the digestive system. Constipation is often linked to skin problems, so good digestion is important.

Caffeine

Caffeine increases the levels of stress hormones in the body, and it is thought to stimulate sebum production. Caffeine can be found in cola, chocolate and fizzy drinks, as well as coffee.

Foods considered beneficial for acne

The healthiest foods to eat for your skin include fruit, vegetables, nuts and seeds, as they are full of all the necessary vitamins and minerals you need. These foods help the skin regenerate while at the same time protecting it from free radicals – harmful molecules in the air – and radiation from ultraviolet rays.

Vitamins

Vitamins may be small but they are vital for performing specific functions that are essential for maintaining health. Research has discovered that people with acne tend to have lower levels of vitamins A and E than normal. Healthy skin requires the vitamins A, C and E in particular. The best way to ensure you have a good supply of vitamins is by eating at least five portions of fruit and vegetables each day (see Table 1).

Vitamin A

This vitamin is also known as retinol, and is one of the most important vitamins for healthy skin and hormonal balance. Vitamin A reduces the production of sebum and is very often found in conventional acne treatments; Retinol-A cream or gel, for example, contains tretinoin, a form of vitamin A. It is also thought vitamin A may help your skin if it is scarred as a result of acne. Good food sources of this vitamin include fish oils, carrots, green leafy vegetables, and yellow and orange fruit such as peppers, mangoes and peaches. High doses of vitamin A can be toxic, so if you intend to take a vitamin supplement do not exceed the manufacturer's recommended amounts, or consult your doctor.

Important: doses of 25,000 IU or higher of vitamin A should only be taken under professional advice because there is evidence that adverse effects (including birth defects) may result. There are approximately 15,500 IU of vitamin A/100 g of kale and 16,812 IU/100 g of carrots.

Vitamin E

Vitamin E protects your body's cells from free radicals, as it acts as an antioxidant and protects the immune system. Importantly,

Table 1 Acne-friendly vitamin foods

Vitamin A	Carrots, sweet potatoes, 'orange' fruits, mangoes and apricots, nectarines, spinach, broccoli, red peppers, pumpkins, watercress, parsley, melons, tomatoes and red chillies
Vitamin B1 (thiamin)	Oranges, plums, pineapples, cauliflower, kale, garlic, mange tout, leeks, parsley, peas, spinach, bananas, dried fruit, nuts and seeds
Vitamin B2 (riboflavin)	Apricots, asparagus, bananas, blackcurrants, peaches, kale, cherries, broccoli, beansprouts, red peppers, mushrooms, avocados and watercress
Vitamin B3 (niacin)	Grapes, grapefruit, passion fruit, beansprouts, kale, peppers, nuts and seeds, broccoli, carrots, dates, tomatoes, avocados and asparagus
Vitamin B5 (pantothenic acid)	Blackberries, strawberries, broccoli, watermelons, celery, tomatoes, sweet potatoes and chickpeas
Vitamin B6 (pyridoxine)	Blackcurrants, raspberries, watermelons, leeks, green peppers, bananas, avocados and green leafy vegetables
Vitamin B12 (cobalamin)	Found in animal products, such as meat and dairy, but this is not useful if you have reduced dairy products. Very often found in fortified foods such as fortified breakfast cereals. It is much more difficult to find in fruit and vegetables.
Folic acid	Oranges, bananas, pineapples, strawberries, beetroot, spinach, cauliflower, cabbage, broccoli, asparagus, lettuce, chickpeas and sunflower seeds
Biotin	Dark green leafy vegetables, dried fruits and nuts
Vitamin C	Blackcurrants, rose hips, guavas, redcurrants, blackberries, grapefruit, strawberries, kiwi fruit, lemons, oranges, pineapples, broccoli, tomatoes, peppers, leafy green vegetables and watercress
Vitamin D	The main source of this vitamin is sunlight. It is necessary for the absorption of calcium for bones and teeth and is found in minute amounts in oily fish, sunflower seeds, mushrooms and cod liver oil
Vitamin E	Avocados, sweet potatoes, celery, cabbage, watercress, spinach, tofu, nuts and seeds, olives and olive oil
Vitamin K	Brussels sprouts, cabbage, asparagus, spinach, parsley, avocados and kiwi fruit

it regulates vitamin A. Low levels of vitamin A in the body produce toxic effects in the cells, and vitamin E helps to combat these effects. It is also thought to help the skin recover from acne scarring. Good food sources include vegetable oils, wheat-germ, broccoli, peanuts and sunflower seeds.

Vitamin B

There are many B vitamins and together they maintain the health and upkeep of the body's nervous system. They have a direct correlation with stress, depression and anxiety; psychological symptoms associated with acne. These vitamins are water-soluble, so they have to be eaten every day as they cannot be stored in the body. They are also responsible for providing us with energy, which occurs during the conversion of glucose from carbohydrates. The B vitamins most important for acne include

- thiamine (B1)
- riboflavin (B2)
- niacinamide (B3)
- pantothenic acids (B5)
- pyridoxine (B6).

Minerals

Just like vitamins, minerals are essential for a healthy body and skin. Their major functions include converting food into energy, controlling body fluids, and promoting the development of bones and teeth.

They are required in small or minute quantities. Calcium, iron, magnesium, phosphorus, potassium, sodium and sulphur are all found in different food groups, and the trace elements, of which you only need minute amounts, include boron, cobalt, copper, chromium, fluoride, iodine, manganese, selenium, silicon and zinc (see Table 2).

Zinc is thought to play a particularly beneficial role in acne as it transports vitamin A around the body, aids wound healing and inflammation, and is essential for the health of the skin. Zinc is involved in the metabolism of testosterone; a lack of zinc increases the production of testosterone, the precursor for acne. Research has shown zinc to be helpful for up to 60 per cent of those with acne. It can be taken in tablet or cream form, but remember to check if your medication already includes it as it is used with erythromycin, an antibacterial that is available in gel or solution form.

Selenium is another useful mineral. A powerful antioxidant, it protects the skin from harmful free radicals, such as environmental pollution, and radiation from ultraviolet light. Working with vitamins A, C and E, this trace element helps to preserve the skin's elasticity.

Table 2 Food sources for minerals

Sulphur	Onions, raspberries, nuts, cabbage, leafy green vegetables, fish, sweet potatoes, watercress, radishes
Selenium	Garlic, mushrooms, asparagus, lentils, oats, brown rice, brazil nuts, seaweed, avocados, sunflower seeds
Chromium	Brewer's yeast, molasses, wheat bran, whole grains
Zinc	Guavas, raspberries, root vegetables, Brussels sprouts, tomatoes, nuts, pumpkin and sunflower seeds, eggs, seafood, poultry, fortified cereals
Calcium	Kelp, watercress, seeds, sprouted grains, blackberries, raspberries, carrots, kale, celery, dried figs
Iron	Green leafy vegetables, poultry, dried fruit, prunes, blackcurrants, passion fruit, nuts
Magnesium	Seafood, apples, melons, beetroot, peas, spinach, tomatoes, soya, brown rice, figs, strawberries, bananas, peanut butter, potatoes
Phosphorus	Grapes, sesame seeds, fish, lentils, kiwi fruit, parsnips, broccoli
Potassium	Sweet potatoes, bananas, avocados, celery, apricots, cherries, spinach, radishes, watercress, nuts and seeds, peaches
Sodium	Naturally found in nuts, grains, seeds, lemons, melons, celery, beetroot, cabbage, kale, radishes, spinach and watercress

Essential fatty acids

Essential fatty acids (EFAs) support the cardiovascular, reproductive, immune and nervous systems. The human body needs them to manufacture and repair cell membranes and expel harmful waste products. Essential fatty acids make hormonelike substances, prostaglandins, which play an important role in both enhancing and inhibiting the inflammatory response of the body, which as we know is a common condition of acne. Research suggests that people who have low levels of essential fatty acids are more likely to suffer from acne.

The two families of polyunsaturated fats, Omega 3 and Omega 6, cannot be made in the body so they have to be ingested from food. The best foods for these fats include flaxseed oil, flaxseeds, hempseed oil, hempseeds, oily fish including salmon, mackerel, sardines and fresh tuna, seeds, nuts, olive oil, olives and chicken.

Probiotics

Probiotics are healthy digestive bacteria that live in the gut, where they aid digestion and destroy unhealthy bacteria. They can be added to foods and drinks such as yoghurts, are naturally found in some foods like bananas, and are also available as supplements. They are often suggested as a way of helping to maintain a healthy digestive system, as very often an unhealthy digestive system affects the skin.

Chocolate

How many times has someone suggested chocolate has caused your acne? Probably many more times than you care to remember. The good news is that some nutritionists consider dark chocolate that has 70 per cent or more cocoa content useful, because of the anti-inflammatory properties of the flavonoids and antioxidants it contains. These help combat cell damage, which occurs in acne. It is milk chocolate you need to avoid, as this is cocoa combined with sugar, milk powder and/or condensed milk, all guaranteed to affect your hormone production.

Water

Your body is made up of 70 per cent water, and much of it is expelled through the urinary system and sweat. Many of us are regularly dehydrated; common dehydration effects include headaches, lethargy and loss of concentration. Dehydration also slows the skin's natural exfoliation process; dead skin cells stay on the skin's surface for longer and can result in blocked pores, which does not help skin with acne. Very often, dehydration also results in constipation and this further exacerbates skin problems. As toxins build up, they have to be excreted through the skin, triggering the sebaceous glands, inflaming the hair follicles and causing an outbreak of spots.

Not only does drinking water help to keep the body hydrated, but also eating fresh fruit and vegetables helps to provide you with water and fibre. It is not only your skin which will see an improvement from the amount of water you drink: your energy, concentration levels, weight and digestion will all improve too. Sometimes, though, it can be difficult to manage to drink the required amount of water each day – about 2 litres of still water – so some simple tips should help.

- Drink a glass of water first thing every morning. As you normally wake up dehydrated, it's a good start to the day.
- Carry water in a small bottle with you all the time.
- Have water at your desk if you are working.
- Match your other drinks with a glass of water each time.
- Add lemon or lime to your water if you need to flavour it.
- Drink warm or hot water for a change.

Sufficient intake of water will keep you hydrated, aid digestion, promote the healing processes and improve blood circulation, your skin tone and your complexion. It's a cheap and healthy alternative to creams, lotions and potions.

Top tips for healthy skin

- Eat plenty of fruit and vegetables. Government guidelines suggest at least five portions a day.
- Reduce caffeine.
- Reduce saturated fat levels.
- Avoid fried and processed foods.
- Reduce dairy and dairy products for a period of time to see if this has any effect on your acne.
- Reduce refined carbohydrates; choose complex carbohydrates instead.
- Eat nuts and seeds.
- Cut back on sugar and sugar substitutes, such as sweeteners.
- Drink at least 2 litres of still water each day.

9

The psychological effects of acne

There is no single disease which causes more psychic trauma, more maladjustment between parents and children, more general insecurity and feelings of inferiority and greater sums of psychic suffering than does *Acne vulgaris*.

(M. B. Sulzberger and S. H. Zaldems, 1948)

For anyone with *Acne vulgaris* the psychological implications can be devastating, yet it is only in recent times that these effects have been fully appreciated. Doctors and other health professionals now realize that teenagers with acne are the most vulnerable and likely to suffer, as adolescence is a time of significant emotional, physical and social development.

The prevalence of acne can have profound effects, more so than other skin conditions because it is so visible. In a society where the importance of appearance is so great, a person with acne is more likely to suffer from a lack of self-esteem and confidence at some time. Such is its significance that many doctors and dermatologists now consider clinical depression a serious side-effect of acne, and the more severe the acne, the greater the severity of depression. However, depression does significantly reduce when acne is successfully treated, and according to a report in the *Journal of Cutaneous Medicine and Surgery*, the psychological effects of acne should always be taken into account at the beginning of treatment.

There are several aspects of acne which contribute to its psychological effects, including the distribution of spots on the skin, age, social pressures and misconceptions. Acne is usually very obvious, and in most cases it cannot be covered with clothing, so it tends to be on full view. As many teenagers experience acne at a time when they are discovering their own identity and when peer acceptance is very important to them, acne can lead to acute self-consciousness and sensitivity – it does matter what others may think of you.

However, it is not just teenagers who suffer. Adults with acne may also experience feelings of rejection, with loss of self-confidence and self-esteem, especially in the work place. Misconceptions about acne contribute too. According to research in *Dermatology Online Journal*, 30 per cent of acne patients mistakenly believed their acne was caused by poor skin hygiene, and similar beliefs led to feelings of guilt, embarrassment and shame.

Most doctors these days are sympathetic to the feelings experienced by those with acne, and will try to support them through their treatment. However, the degree of psychological distress varies from individual to individual, and it can sometimes be difficult for doctors – and parents and partners – fully to understand your feelings. Make sure you discuss this when you see your doctor, as your psychological health is important, and may even influence your treatment. Don't be surprised if your doctor asks you more questions about your self-esteem and feelings than about your spots in future consultations – he or she needs to know you are coping.

Signs of psychological problems

There are some common signs of psychological distress. Typical signs include:

- low self-esteem or confidence;
- avoiding eye contact;
- girls wanting to wear heavy amounts of make-up;
- growing long hair so it can hang over the face;
- poor body image;
- anger;

- frustration;
- staying away from – or making excuses to avoid – swimming and other sports where you need to change in front of others or expose your skin, especially if you suffer from acne on the body;
- bullying – others, especially teenagers, may be quick to mock those with acne by name-calling or exclusion from peer groups;
- relationship difficulties;
- refusing to attend school;
- refusing to go to work;
- taking sick days and jeopardizing employment;
- limiting work choices – for example, excluding jobs where you meet and greet the public and image is important;
- depression;
- anxiety.

Some of these reactions are just part of normal experience, but if you feel they're causing undue distress or becoming very pronounced, do make an appointment with your doctor.

Helping yourself

Remember, you are not alone. At any one time, more than 90 per cent of teenagers have acne, while 30 per cent of the general population suffer from acne. Acne doesn't discriminate; it doesn't care about your gender, background, education or financial status. But the good news is that acne treatments will and can help, and the sooner you treat your acne, the quicker your acne will respond.

Depression

Depression usually builds up over time, but it can also take a while before you or someone around you realizes you are depressed. If you do feel down, anxious or depressed about your acne, then make sure you make an appointment to see your doctor and discuss the way you feel. The Acne Support Group suggests around 12 per cent of people with acne will feel suicidal, but acne does not have to go untreated. If your acne is being treated with isotretinoin then there is a chance you may become depressed, a side-effect of this particular drug. If this is the case, or you think it may be, then make sure you see your doctor or dermatologist immediately.

Signs of depression include:

- loss of appetite
- moodiness
- behavioural problems
- lethargy
- crying
- lack of self-confidence
- reduced quality of life.

Any parent of a teenager will know how common it is for adolescents to retreat to their bedroom, and mood swings, irritability, feeling up and then down are very common during these years. However, teenagers with acne may suffer from depression, and may not only spend long hours in their bedroom but also withdraw socially from both family and friends. They may suffer at school; grades can go down, or they become uninterested in their studies and start to fall behind in schoolwork. If you think this is happening then seek medical help, book an appointment with your doctor, and also inform the school. Your child's teacher or tutor, school nurse or counsellor may be able to offer some help and advice.

Don't let your teenager suffer from acne for any longer than necessary: make sure the acne treatment is appropriate and be certain to follow all instructions correctly. Also try and ensure your teenager attends follow-up appointments with the doctor to evaluate the treatment and its success. If you really think treatment is not working then encourage him or her to ask for it to be changed. Being supportive during these difficult years will be challenging but your child needs to know you are always there to help.

Treatment for depression

There are a variety of medical treatments that your doctor may advise, and thankfully depression can nearly always be treated effectively. You may be prescribed antidepressant tablets, such as Prozac, or counselling, which can help build confidence and self-esteem. Group therapy may also be offered, or the contact details and introduction to a self-help group.

If you are suffering from depression, there are a number of ways you can help yourself:

- Get out every day in the fresh air.
- Take up exercise. It can be as simple as going for a walk or a cycle ride. This is something you can do on your own if you really want to, but doing it in company is more sociable.
- Eat a healthy diet. Make sure you get your necessary vitamins and minerals and your essential fatty acids.
- Take a vitamin B supplement to increase serotonin levels, a hormone responsible for mood. Low levels of serotonin are known to cause depression.
- Have a massage. It will help you to relax.
- Take up a new hobby.
- You can take St John's Wort as a natural antidepressant, but if you are taking any other form of medication check with your doctor first.
- Try yoga, Tai Chi or relaxation classes.
- Make sure you get adequate sleep.
- Cut back on alcohol and caffeine.

Dysmorphophobic acne

In rare cases, some people who suffer from mild acne may have a disproportionate view of themselves and think they are suffering from severe acne. This perception affects their body image, and they may suffer from psychological and social symptoms. Dysmorphophobic acne usually requires medical treatment, and isotretinoin therapy may be prescribed on a low-dose, long-term basis. In the worst cases this is a body image disorder, similar to anorexia nervosa.

Acne myths and misconceptions

There are many misconceptions about acne. Doctors and dermatologists are often surprised to find that their patients believe many of these misconceptions. Unfortunately, such mistaken beliefs can unnecessarily increase feelings of anxiety and guilt in those with acne.

The most common include:

- *Acne is caused through bad hygiene and dirty skin.* This is simply not true. Blackheads are the colour they are through oxidization, not dirt.
- *Washing more will help.* No, it won't – in fact, you will probably make your acne worse, as you are likely to irritate the skin with all that scrubbing. However, if you do not wash your face at all, and leave make-up on your skin, you are likely to encourage bacteria to multiply.
- *There is no cure for acne.* There are several very effective treatments for acne, which can keep your spots under control.
- *A suntan will improve acne.* This is not true either, as you are more likely to dry your skin, increase your wrinkles and age your skin. However, the most important concern is that you may increase your risk of skin cancer.
- *Covering your spots with make-up will help.* To an extent this is

correct, but only if you use non-comedogenic products and you don't suffer from moderate to severe acne.

- *Sex or masturbation causes acne.* Simply not true, but acne is linked to the sex hormones, in particular testosterone.
- *Fatty foods and chocolate cause acne.* You need to read Chapter 8.
- *Only teenagers have acne.* No, they don't! From babies to adults, acne can affect anyone, regardless of age.
- *Acne is a contagious disease.* No, it isn't. You cannot catch acne or pass it from one person to another.
- *Acne appears only on the face.* Another misconception: acne can appear on other parts of the body too, the most common being the back, shoulders, chest, arms and neck.
- *Squeezing spots will clear them up.* This might be tempting, but in some cases can lead to scarring, pocks and holes in the skin. Better to have a spot for a few days than a scar for life.
- *All acne medications are the same.* No, they are not. See Chapter 4.
- *Acne can disappear overnight.* Unfortunately not: acne can take weeks, months and in some cases years to treat, but it can be controlled with medication.
- *Acne is simply a cosmetic condition.* No, not true: acne is recognized as having psychological and physical implications.

Supporting someone with acne

Very often, the person most likely to be supporting someone with acne is a parent. However, if your partner has developed acne, for whatever reason – pregnancy, stress or hormonal activity – it is worthwhile understanding what you can do to help.

Learning as much as possible about the condition, type of acne and treatment is useful. If the person is not using any medication, then do suggest that he or she consults a doctor, as it is so important for acne to be treated as early as possible.

You may need to reinforce the idea that the acne is not a direct result of something the person has done, or is doing, and that he or she has nothing to feel guilty about. Keep a close look-out for any signs of anxiety or depression. Teenagers in particular are difficult to monitor, as they can often be moody and irritable and suffer mood swings, but try and encourage frank discussion of their feelings when they are in a good mood. Acne is difficult to live with, whether you are a teenager or an adult, but having someone who supports you and loves you for what you are, and not how you look, is the biggest support you can give and they can have.

10

Planning a treatment path

Many people with acne will tell you that one of the worst things about their condition is that it is literally 'in your face'. There is not a day when you don't get up and rush to the mirror to see if the spots have gone. It can be difficult sometimes to remain optimistic when your skin is affected with red inflamed spots, blackheads or whiteheads, and at times it may affect your self-esteem and confidence. Having a treatment plan in place helps you to stay in control of your acne, and not your acne in control of you.

The most important step towards managing your acne is to make sure you treat it as soon as possible. Successful acne management is all about what works for you, your skin and your type of acne. What may cure your friend's acne may not work for you at all; in fact it may even irritate your skin further. You could find you have to try several treatments before you find the most suitable for your skin.

Choosing your treatment is a personal decision based upon the advice you receive from your doctor. Keep your expectations realistic. All too often doctors see people with acne coming back to them, only to discover they didn't continue with their medication.

Emotions too have a role to play in the treatment of acne. Anger, resentment, anxiety, frustration and depression are all very common, and you may even suffer from physical pain or itching, headaches, lethargy and fatigue. At times you will need support from friends and family, and maybe professional support from your doctor, consultant or a support group. All of them can help you feel much more confident about your condition and your treatment plan. The Internet can provide information and online support, and if you are at school or college the health advisor or nurse may be able to help too. Don't feel you have to deal with your acne on your own: the more support you receive, the more successful your management of your acne will be. Acne requires you to take some very positive steps and actions to find a treatment that works well for you and your skin.

Don't be fooled

There are many products on the market offering overnight acne success and a few may work, but for the majority there is no such thing as a quick acne fix. You are likely to find that even the best acne treatments take several weeks, if not months, to make any noticeable difference. Acne can be managed and controlled, but you may have to be prepared for it to take time, and many will not realize that acne can flare up again once you stop treatment – you may find you have to carry on with a 'maintenance' treatment plan for several years if necessary in order to prevent another break-out. This is very often the experience many teenagers will have, treating their spots until they are into their mid-twenties. A low-level dose of benzoyl peroxide or a topical retinoid is often used for maintenance treatments, so if you have been using antibiotics for your acne you may have to change to another treatment option, as long-term antibiotic use is not desirable.

Many dermatologists often feel that their patients have unrealistic expectations regarding treatment, and are disillusioned when there are no significant changes within a few weeks. Often these people cease treatment on the grounds that it isn't working, not realizing just how long it takes for the benefits to be seen. It can be difficult to remain cheerful and positive if your treatment isn't working as quickly as you would like, but your doctor can help if you find it too depressing. Acne can be difficult and may cause you some misery, but you mustn't give up trying to find the right solution for you: there will be one.

Drawing up a plan

Chapter 4 gives you information on the types of conventional treatments available for acne. Determining if your treatment is working is important, and the easiest way to keep track of your progress is by drawing up a table or monitoring chart. It can be as simple as you like; the main objective is to establish changes in your acne.

Remember, you may experience new outbreaks before your acne begins to clear, which is why it is important to allow time for the treatment to work. It is all too easy to get disheartened and to change treatments too quickly without really giving them a chance to work.

A monitoring chart like Table 3 works well on a weekly schedule. Write down the treatment you use, and if you miss a day, record this. Note the acne washes, creams and medication used. Now count the actual number of blackheads, whiteheads and any red bumps you have. Start on one side of your face and finish on the other – it's a good idea to always start in the same place. If you are covered in spots then you can round up, or estimate, the number you have. Then record the number of acne lesions on your chart. At first you will be counting the same spots, until your treatment starts to work.

If you can see no improvements after four to six weeks from when you started the treatment, consider changing to a new regime. Continue with the chart. This is the most effective way of knowing what is or isn't working for you. Don't keep on with a treatment if you find it is irritating your skin or making it sore, and if you are using prescription treatment then make sure you see your doctor or dermatologist if you want to stop or change treatments.

If you think certain foods are causing your skin to react, keeping a food chart of all the food you eat and drink in a day may help you to see an emerging pattern, and you can eliminate suspects from your diet.

Table 3 Acne monitoring chart

Date	No. of blackheads	No. of whiteheads	No. of red bumps	Treatment used
Monday				
Tuesday				
Wednesday				
Thursday				
Friday				
Saturday				
Sunday				

Professional treatment plan

Your doctor or dermatologist will decide upon the treatment he or she thinks is most suitable, but make sure you discuss it thoroughly beforehand. You need to understand what is being offered, your expectations and any side-effects that may occur. The doctor may take into account previous treatment and any scarring you may have. Some doctors may ask you to fill out a questionnaire, known as an Assessment of Psychological Effects of Acne (APSEA), which assesses the psychological and social effects acne is having on you. The Cardiff Acne Disability Index (CADI) is another questionnaire, usually used for teenagers and young adults, and the Dermatology Quality of Life Index (DQLI) is usually used for adults. Other grading systems include the Cook Method, which uses grading photographs, and the Pillsbury Scale.

Poor response to treatment

Generally, most dermatologists agree that the main reason for a poor response to treatment is because the person has not used or taken it every day. Having to apply cream to your skin or use antibiotics every day for months may seem tedious, but the minute you break the treatment cycle then the chances are the bacteria will start to multiply and your skin will break out in spots. If you are struggling to use your treatment, go back to your doctor and discuss it with him or her.

At times when you are under a lot of stress, such as during exams, you may find that your treatment doesn't work as effectively. At times like these you may find relaxation or stress management techniques can help, and hopefully the stress won't last too long.

Research into acne

Since the development of the drug isotretinoin over ten years ago, there has been very little development in new acne treatments. Although skin specialists understand the factors that create an acne outbreak, they are still far from understanding or finding out exactly what is required to stop acne from occurring, and for that reason there is no one successful cure. However, research from Hammersmith Hospital under consultant dermatologist Professor Tony Chu is exciting. His research into molecular events which cause acne is ongoing, and he believes new acne treatments are beginning to evolve. As for when they will be available, he is not yet sure, but he and his team are committed to providing natural acne treatments and solutions.

In the United States, researchers from Harvard Medical School and Dr Anderson from Massachusetts General Hospital have developed a new laser technique, which they believe could be a revolutionary new treatment for acne. The free-electron laser (FEL) produces very specific beams of light that heat and break down fat without damaging other body tissue. Researchers are now looking into the possibility of a particular laser wavelength directly targeting sebaceous glands and isolating the source of spots. Research is ongoing, but so far Dr Anderson is both excited and hopeful about the results.

Other research closer to home has discovered that anti-oxidants are useful in treating those with severe *Acne vulgaris* and recommends that drugs that treat acne should have anti-oxidative effects. There are many so-called 'superfoods', such as blueberries, that contain antioxidants and have antioxidant effects upon the cells in the body, so eating a diet rich in anti-oxidants may be another useful resource in the fight against acne.

And finally ...

Acne is one of the most debilitating skin conditions to affect most of the population. It usually strikes at the time when your life is changing, when social, physical and psychological chal-lenges are appearing, and your spots cause you grief and stress. But there is light at the end of the tunnel: you just have to find what works for you, and that may mean having to live with your spots for a while. There is no such thing as perfect skin, apart from in glossy magazines: real human beings have skin that is blemished or wrinkled or misshapen, with broken noses or bushy eyebrows and spots. Don't give up – it might take ages and several attempts, but eventually there will be a treatment that works for you and your skin.

Useful addresses

The Acne Support Group
Howard House
The Runway
South Ruislip
Middlesex HA4 6SE
Tel.: 0208 561 6868
Website: www.stopspots.org.uk

AcuMedic Clinic
101–105 Camden High Street
(Headquarters)
London NW1 7JN
Tel.: 020 7388 6704
Website: www.acumedic.com

A long-established clinic for
traditional Chinese medicine, with
another branch in Bath (01225 483
393).

Avene Dermatological Spa
Tel.: 00 33 0 467 23 41 87
Website: www.
avenehydrotherapycenter.com

Spring water and other treatments
have been used for more than 200
years to treat skin conditions at
this spa in south-western France.

BeautySkin
Goldstaff Ltd
Hexgreave Hall
Farnsfield
Newark NG22 8LS
Tel.: 01623 884303l; 0800 1388 567
(freephone; 8 a.m. to 9 p.m., seven
days a week)
Website: www.beautyskinuk.co.uk

British Acupuncture Council
63 Jeddo Road
London W12 9HQ
Tel.: 020 8735 0400
Website: www.acupuncture.org.uk

**British Association of
Dermatologists**
Willan House
4 Fitzroy Square
London W1T 5HQ
Tel.: 020 7383 0266
Website: www.bad.org.uk

British Autogenic Society
Royal London Homoeopathic
Hospital
Great Ormond Street
London WC1N 3HR
Tel.: 020 7391 8908
Website: www.autogenic-therapy.
co.uk

Provides information about
autogenic training, which is a
simple self-help technique for stress
management and relaxation.

British Homeopathic Association
Hahnemann House
29 Park Street West
Luton LU1 3BE
Tel.: 0870 444 3950
Website: www.trusthomeopathy.org

British Nutrition Foundation
High Holborn House
52–54 High Holborn
London WC1V 6RQ
Tel.: 020 7404 6504
Website: www.nutrition.org.uk

British Red Cross
Tel.: 0844 871 11 11 (office); 0844
412 2804 (general enquiries)
Website: www.redcross.org.uk

British Skin Foundation
4 Fitzroy Square
London W1T 5HQ
Tel.: 020 7391 6341
Website: www.
britishskinfoundation.org.uk

British Wheel of Yoga
Tel.: 01529 306851
Website: www.bwy.org.uk

Relaxing therapies such as yoga
will not cure your acne but are
helpful in reducing stress.

Changing Faces
The Squire Centre
33–37 University Street
London WC1E 6JN
Tel.: 0845 4500 275 (Northern
Ireland 0845 4500 732; Scotland
0845 4500 640; Wales 0845 4500
240)
Website: www.changingfaces.org.uk

Hammersmith Hospital
Du Cane Road
London W12 0HS
Tel.: 020 8383 1000
Website: www.imperial.nhs.uk/
hammersmith

**National Institute of Medical
Herbalists**
Tel.: 01392 426022
Website: www.nimh.org.uk

NHS Direct
Helpline: 0845 46 47 (24 hours)
Website: www.nhsdirect.nhs.uk

**NHS Skin Disorders Specialist
Library**
Website: www.library.nhs.uk/skin/

**Royal London Homoeopathic
Hospital**
60 Great Ormond Street
London WC1N 3HR
Tel.: 020 7391 8888 (patient
services)
Website: www.uclh.nhs.uk (click on
'Our hospitals')

Skin Laser Directory
Website: www.skinlaserdirectory.
org.uk/Directory.htm

SkinMed
Whitestacks House
Havikil Lane
Scotton
Harrogate
North Yorkshire HG5 9HN
Tel.: 08701 909 369
Website: www.skinmed.co.uk

Index